Enterprise Java Applications Architecture on VMware

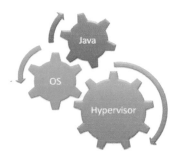

Emad Benjamin

ISBN: 0615507883
ISBN-13: 9780615507880

Contents

Acknowledgements

I would like to first thank my wife Christine, and our wonderful children Anthony and Adrian, for their understanding on not spending enough time with them, while I was writing this book. For my wife in particular, who is the pillar of my strength - always inspiring, understanding, and accommodating.

I also want to thank my parents George and Najia for the sacrifices they have made so that I can pursue my education, and career.

I would also like to express my gratitude to Christine's parents Robert, and Eileen and her brother Rameil for all their support and encouragement.

I would like to acknowledge Raj Ramanujam, director of global technical solutions and services team at VMware, who inspired me to write this book, and for his constant support in helping me further my knowledge on VMware products. Raj is always encouraging the team of experts that he leads to share their knowledge with the community, both at VMware and with VMware customers. I am privileged to work in the technical solutions team under his motivational style of leadership.

I would also like to thank my colleague Justin Murray, Java evangelist at VMware, who has been a pleasure to work with and is the original author of the first version of VMware's best-practices paper on running Java on vSphere.

Many thanks to my colleague, Hal Rosenberg, senior performance engineer at VMware, for his outstanding performance testing of Java workloads, and his generosity in allowing the use of his work in Chapter 9.

I would like to thank my colleague Steve Jin, senior engineer at VMware, for his phenomenal work on the VI Java API, and the many good examples he has written.

I would like to thank Yvonne Wassenaar, VP of Strategy and GTS at VMware; Matt Stepanski, VP of GTS at VMware; Jennifer Heublein, Sr. Director of Sales Enablement at VMware; and Bret Bechis from VMware legal for their support in approving this book.

To other colleagues who have contributed to the Java on VMware domain over the years – it has been a blessing and an honor to have worked with such an outstanding team:
Ole Agesen, John Arrasjid, Allan Burnett, Shruti Bhat, Dan Carwin, Gaetan Castelein, Blake Connell, Ben Corrie, Melissa Cotton, Scott Deeg, Duncan Epping, Jamie Engesser, Alex Fontana, Filip Hanik, Ross Knippel, Gilbert Lau, Gideon Low, Kannan Mani, Steve Mayzak, Vas Mitra, David McJannet, Matt Quinlan, Scott Salyer, Lise Storc, My Tran, James Williams, and Matthew Wood.

To the team at VMware IT, a big round of thanks for the many times that we achieved great success in Virtualizing Java:
Daryl Bauza, Michael Caulfield, Len Ceruzzi, Chan Chi, John Davis, Jason Deglau, Bill Heil, Jeremy Hunt, Shawn Holland, Rick Lindberg, Grant Noel, Bill O'Hare, Bob Plummer, Leo Remizov, Joe Roche, Amit Singh, Travis Sween, David Ta, and Andrew Woodward.

Last, but not least, special thanks to Jun Yang, senior engineer at Google, for the numerous times that we spent improving how Java application ought to be developed and deployed, and the Cornerstone framework that we co-authored while at Cisco. Much of that work placed the seeds for a lot of the tuning that I was able to apply in later years.

About the Author

Emad Benjamin has been in the IT industry for the past twenty years. He graduated with a Bachelor of Electrical Engineering from the University of Wollongong. Earlier in his career, he was a C++ software engineer, then in 1997, he switched to programming with Java, and has been focusing on Java ever since. He has extensive software development experience with companies such as, Cisco, Oracle, Citadel, BHP Steel, and others. For the past seven years, his main focus has been Java on VMware vSphere. Emad is currently at VMware focusing on all aspects of Virtualizing Java. He has presented at many conferences and workshops around the world on the topic of Virtualizing Java, where he has shared his experience and best practices.

You can connect with Emad on LinkedIn at:
http://www.linkedin.com/in/emadbenjamin

Dedication

I dedicate this book to my beloved wife Christine, and our two beautiful boys Anthony and Adrian. They fill our life with plenty of joy.

Abstract

This book is the culmination of seven years of experience in running Java on VMware vSphere, both at VMware and at many of VMware's customer sites. In fact, many of VMware's customers run business critical enterprise Java applications on VMware vSphere where they have achieved better TCO and SLAs. This book covers high-level architecture and implementation details, such as design and sizing, high-availability designs, automation of deployments, best practices, tuning, and troubleshooting techniques of enterprise Java applications on VMware.

Chapter 1

Introduction

1.1 Motivation

I spent the last seven years at VMware in various capacities ensuring that all internal enterprise Java applications at VMware were virtualized in order to showcase to VMware customers the benefits of the approach. I came to the realization that a lot of the best practices that we learned from empirical evidence in production would be very useful to share in the community. I received lots of feedback requesting that I document many of the lessons learned and the various tips and tricks needed to successfully run enterprise Java applications on VMware. Hence this book!

But before you dive into the book, keep something in mind. While it has been a great learning experience that yielded many best practices presented in this book, the best practices are really for optimal configuration guidance as opposed to mandatory requirements. We found that most enterprise Java applications virtualize readily without having to worry about too many specific configurations. In fact, of any enterprise-level production application, Java applications are prime low-hanging-fruit candidates for virtualization.

Predominantly, the lessons learned fell into the following categories:
⇨ Things will go wrong in production, and it is just a matter of when. So it is advisable to take a meticulous approach about what could go wrong and plan a roll-forward and roll-back plan. The planning exercise helps in further solidifying the QA test plan. NOTE: This is not specific to a virtualized environment; in fact it is an equally stringent requirement whether you are dealing with a physical and/or virtual infrastructure. However, the reality is that

virtualization gives you an advantage with flexibility mechanisms that you can use to quickly deal with issues as opposed to in a physical case where you are restricted to the amount of flexibility with moving compute resources around.

⇨ Enterprise Java applications are the low-hanging fruit when it comes to virtualization

⇨ Everyone operated in various silos at each of the Java tiers and did not necessarily speak the same language in terms of technology and organizational logistics

⇨ Cross-team collaboration was a big part of our effort to virtualize Java on VMware. It drove a lot of the teams to talk to each other in order to facilitate a best-of-breed design. Teams from both sides of application development and operations came to the table many times.

Over the last couple of years I have seen an increase in the adoption of Virtualizing Java-application servers, and many of the questions we have come across are documented in this book. This book provides an architectural perspective needed to effectively run enterprise Java applications on VMware, and it is also a collection of lessons learned from running serious production Java workloads on VMware.

Finally, one of the main motivations was the fact that we found Java application developers who knew the development process really well, knew how to write Java code, and knew how to tune the JVM. That information stayed with developers and did not necessarily translate all the way to the administrators of the application. Often, we found the skills needed to run Java on VMware was split between Java developers and VMware administrators, but not a single person knew both. Over time we helped grow the notion of a single professional who understood how to write Java code, deploy it, tune the JVM, and recognized the full breadth of virtualization. I believe this motivation will help grow an industry of professionals who will follow this career path and skill-set profile.

The above is what motivated me to put it all together in one book. I hope it will be helpful to professionals with backgrounds in Java development, operations infrastructure, and virtualization. The book is designed to be a tool for combating day-to-day situations, but it also is to be used in composing a strategic architectural map of your virtualized Java platform. I hope it inspires others to follow a professional career based on the skills needed to run virtualized enterprise Java applications as experts who can combine their Java knowledge with VMware.

1.2 Target Audience

This book is targeted at IT professionals who are in search of implementation guidelines for running enterprise Java applications on VMware vSphere in production, and QA/Test environments.

The first three chapters are beneficial to CIOs, VPs, directors, and enterprise architects looking for key high-level business propositions of Virtualizing enterprise Java applications. The remaining chapters are for developers and administrators looking for implementation details.

1.3 Prerequisites

A high-level understanding of virtualization technology is assumed in this book. This book is based on running enterprise Java on VMware vSphere, which is bare metal hypervisor virtualization. While a recommendation to read about virtualization is appropriate, most senior Java specialists will quickly ascertain enough about virtualization and Virtualizing Java applications from this book. In fact, by reading the answer to the following question you can get enough of a background on virtualization to continue through this book. This is the question asked on day one of folks new to Virtualizing Java: "Is Java both OS and hypervisor independent?"

1.3.1 Is Java both OS and Hypervisor Independent?

For those who don't really have time to read the entire section, the answer is simply, "Yes," to the above question. Indeed, Java is independent of the underlying hypervisor, such as VMware's bare metal hypervisor, and the operating system. But for those who want to delve a little more into what this means, please read on.

This question has recently surfaced from those who are new to virtualization, and not so new to Java. Now while the answer to the question posed was candidly obvious, it was a legitimate question to address, as it seemed to have been asked a few times.

There is no doubt that Java's main design tenets are based on a cross-platform language that is operating systems independent, so long as there is an operating-system-supported underlying runtime. We know this runtime as the Java Virtual Machine (JVM) that has become a permanent fixture of many enterprise application platforms. You could write a Java application and run it on various JVMs on different operating systems, and without needing to recompile. Now of course many of VMware's customers have one vendor-targeted JVM in production, and wouldn't have to worry about moving a Java application from one JVM implementation to another. But if they chose to do so, they could easily do it, primarily due to Java's cross-platform and operating system independence facilitated by a JVM.

Hence, you can conclude that the Java applications don't really care which JVM is being targeted to run on and are independent of the specific JVM implementation and operating system.

Of course some of you may say "What about all of the different internal behaviors of one JVM versus another?" At the end of the day they all adhere to the JVM spec, and while some JVM options (-XX, flags, etcetera) are named differently, they more or less behave in a similar manner. Certainly the differences are not in the language, but in the way the Java process can be optimized with various JVM options passed at the Java command line.

Now fast forward to the infrastructure side of things. VMware ESXi is a bare metal hypervisor that makes it possible to run multiple operating systems on a particular piece of hardware. It alleviates the infrastructure administrators from having to worry about installing one kind of operating system for one piece of hardware versus another. VMware makes the operating system run independent of the underlying hardware (bare metal) and creates a degree of independence between the operating system and the bare metal/ hardware.

While the answer to the question of "Is Java both OS and hypervisor independent?" is clearly yes, it is due to two degrees of independence. The first degree is that of Java's main tenet of cross-platform and OS independence, and the second degree is that of VMware ESXi hypervisor making the operating system independent of the hardware that it runs on. In fact, when a Java application runs on an operating system that is in an ESXi-based virtual machine, ESXi has no notion of knowing it is a Java workload running on the operating system, making the ESX hypervisor completely independent of the workload that is running on it. A further testament to this is when you deploy a Java application on a virtual machine, no operating-system changes are needed due to this independence.

Conversely, the JVM doesn't really know that it is running on a virtual machine sitting on an ESXi hypervisor, and to the JVM, the VM appears like any other server with compute resources (CPUs, RAM, etcetera) presented to it.

In conclusion, so long as the JVM you are using is supported on the operating system that your applications are running on, there is no need for additional concern and/or dependency for additional support from the downstream virtual machine and ESXi layers.

The following diagram, in Figure 1, illustrates all the layers we discussed in answering the question posed in this section.

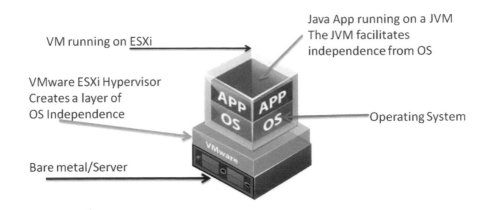

Java App running on a JVM
The JVM facilitates
independence from OS

VM running on ESXi

VMware ESXi Hypervisor
Creates a layer of
OS Independence

Operating System

Bare metal/Server

Figure 1: *Shows an enterprise Java application running on a VM virtualized by VMware ESXi*

1.4 Overview

This book is split into twelve chapters. Chapter 2 is a high-level introduction to the motivation behind running enterprise Java applications on VMware vSphere, while chapters 3 through 12 are the various implementations details.

- Chapter 2: Why Virtualize Enterprise Java Applications? — This chapter answers why virtualize enterprise Java applications. Enterprise Java applications are cross-platform and can be moved from one OS to another with relative ease, as long as the guest OS has a supported JVM that can run on the guest operating system.

- Chapter 3: Enterprise Java Applications on VMware— this chapter highlights the applicable use cases of enterprise Java application requirements for dynamic scalability, rapid provisioning, and high availability, which are growing concerns for development and operations groups today. Achieving these requirements with platforms that are completely based on conventional hardware is complex and expensive. Virtualization is a breakthrough technology that alleviates the pressures that common enterprise Java applications requirements may impose on an organization. Features such as horizontal scalability, vertical scalability, rapid provisioning, enhanced high availability, and business continuance are some of the key attributes that are available with the VMware vSphere™ suite.

- Chapter 4: Design and Sizing of Enterprise Java on VMware— this chapter highlights key considerations and provides guidelines to IT architects who are in the process of sizing their enterprise Java applications to run on VMware vSphere™. Our objective is to give guidance on how to obtain the best sizing configuration for your Java applications running on VMware vSphere. You are guided through the process of performance benchmarking on an application, and given pointers on what to measure, what is available to be tuned, and how to best determine the optimal size for your Java application.

- Chapter 5: High-availability Designs of Enterprise Java on VMware— this chapter addresses several dimensions of the high-availability architecture of enterprise Java applications on VMware, including the following:
  o Ability to perform zero-downtime (seamless) application releases during scheduled maintenance
  o Ability to handle traffic bursts and maintain adequate SLAs
  o Ability to perform effective disaster recovery

- Chapter 6: Enterprise Java on VMware Best Practices— this chapter provides information about best practices for deploying enterprise Java applications on VMware, including key best-practice considerations for architecture, performance, design and sizing, and high availability. This information is intended to help IT architects successfully deploy and run Java environments on VMware vSphere™.

- Chapter 7: UNIX-to-Linux Migration Considerations— this chapter focuses on key considerations for IT architects who are in the process of migrating Java applications from UNIX to Linux as part of their VMware server-consolidation project. Now due to Java's cross-platform portability, Java applications are prime candidates to be migrated first with relatively low complexity and effort. Constraints mentioned in this chapter are applicable for Java applications that migrate from one OS to another, regardless of whether they run on physical or virtualized machines—they are not limits imposed by virtualization. The Java application code and runtime paradigm do not change when you migrate to a virtualized system. In fact, a Java application or application WAR file can be deployed as is from its physical machine form onto a Virtual Machine (VM) without any change.

- Chapter 8: Run Effectively in Production— this chapter focuses on lesson learned and what high-level techniques and processes can be implemented to produce more robust, scalable, and highly available enterprise Java applications that run on vSphere.

- Chapter 9: Performance Study— this chapter summarizes some of the key highlights from a performance study paper published by a colleague at VMware, senior performance engineer Harold Rosenberg.

- Chapter 10: Application Modernization and vFabric— this chapter looks at components in vFabric and considers how to best modernize certain aspects of application architecture. We also take a slight deeper dive into vFabric GemFire as this now proves to be a critical component of the role of data, and particularly distributed data, in the cloud.

- Chapter 11: Troubleshooting Primer— this chapter summarizes what to do when you hit a bottleneck or a performance issue while Virtualizing Java, It is a very helpful summary often used out in the field.

- Chapter 12: FAQ—Enterprise Java Applications on vSphere— this chapter is a collection of the many questions from VMware customers that I have encountered over the years. I think is always helpful to quickly ramp up on any technology by reading FAQs.

Chapter 2

Why Virtualize Enterprise Java Applications

2.1 Why VMware vSphere and Java?

With the proliferation of Web-based applications over the past fifteen years, and in particular Web 2.0 over the last five years, increasingly we find that Java is used for most of these applications. This evolution is in direct response to consumers and enterprises seeking to do more on the Web and add more functionality to their applications, which are presented to users via a Web browser interface.

Developers need to rapidly create applications due to this accelerated Web growth, and to accomplish this they need a flexible programming language like Java and a set of complementary dynamic Web languages. However, due to the rapid growth of the Web, architects and developers found the majority of their time consumed with endless performance, scalability and high-availability issues in the production environment. In response, IT operations typically over-provisioned in anticipation of the unknown and thus added to costs, or informed IT developers to wait until hardware could be acquired and provisioned, which often involved long lead times. The gap between the needs of the IT developers and the ability of IT operations to provide infrastructure persisted in physical environments.

IT operations sought to reduce this gap and meet the needs created by the growth of the Web and Java. They looked for solutions that offered more malleability in the datacenter, and quickly embraced virtualization. Virtualization offers the ability to improve utilization of hardware resources, quickly provision compute resources, manage power costs more effectively due to less over-provisioning, and provide ease of administration and higher availability. At the same time, it relieved architects and developers from having to worry so much about scalability and availability, and allowed them to focus on application logic.

You can draw a parallel timeline between the growth of the Web and Java, and the growth of virtualization. Virtualization quickly matured in response to the ever-increasing demand of traffic loads from Web-based applications that datacenters had to handle. Virtualization permits creation of the elastic datacenter so that Web and Java applications can handle massive traffic loads. In particular, VMware vSphere has been at the forefront by providing key features such as better utilization, higher availability, improved scalability, and disaster recovery.

Web and Java applications deployed on VMware vSphere are a great match. VMware has made a strategic commitment to the Java community with its acquisition of SpringSource, and it plans to consolidate these technologies, not only by supporting Java on a vSphere stack, but also by advancing the journey into a cloud offering. In many ways, the cloud is the answer to the pains that Java developers have endured. VMware vSphere solutions made available to the Java community have helped drive down costs, and they further enable Java developer productivity to rapidly deliver scalable and highly available applications.

VSphere specifically offers the following features:

Server consolidation:-
- Utilize all your server processor cores.
- Maintain role isolation without additional hardware expense.

Operational advantages:-
- Design for today's workload rather than guessing about tomorrow.
- Design for specific business requirements.

- Rapidly provision Java servers with virtual machine templates.
- Reduce hardware and operational costs of maintaining a Java lab.
- Enhance testing and troubleshooting using cloned production virtual machines.

Higher availability with less complexity:-
- Reduce planned downtime due to hardware or BIOS updates with VMware VMotion™.
- Reduce unplanned downtime due to hardware failure or resource constraints.
- Implement simple and reliable Java disaster recovery.

2.2 Overview of Java-based Application Architecture

Enterprise Java application architectures are comprised of the following tiers:

Load Balancer Tier—uses various load-balancing algorithms to distribute user traffic among the Web servers.

The Web Server Tier—handles static content processing and in turn, sends request for dynamic content to the assigned application server that houses the Java process.

Java Application Tier (Java Process)—sends the user transaction to the data tier, and it executes any additional Java business logic on the data to prepare for presentation back to the calling client. This is the Java process inside the application server.

Database Tier—stores information about the transaction for later retrieval. This is typically a relational database or any other data store.

In Figure 2, the four main tiers of a conventional enterprise Java application are shown, with each tier having a design and implementation impact on the next tier during a change, as indicated by the brown arrows that permeate the boundaries between the tiers.

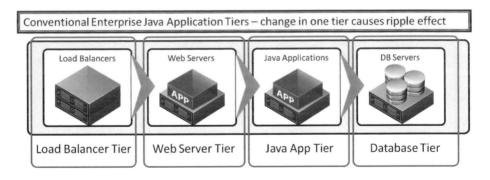

Figure 2: *Shows multiple tiers of conventional enterprise Java applications*

2.3 Key Challenges of Conventional Java Enterprise Application Architecture

Over-provisioning of Compute Resources:

Because traffic demand can vary immensely, depending on the popularity of the enterprise Java   application being deployed, it becomes difficult for the IT development organization to set the right requirements with IT operations. In turn, IT operations often have to over-provision to accommodate for the worst-case scenario.

Slow Acquisition and Deployment of Compute Resources:

Enterprise Java applications built on conventional, physical-hardware architecture are always difficult to change as all the layers have a tight hardware dependency. A change in any one of the tiers often results In a rIpple effect of changes on other layers, and affects uptime metrics and the agility needed for rapid releases.

Software Upgrades and Enterprise Java Application Releases Result in Downtime:

If the operating system is running on conventional hardware, changes often cannot be performed in isolation. Also, the lack of ability to incrementally release software to each server instance without affecting application uptime poses a great challenge for meeting the increasing demands of the ever-evolving Web.

Expectation Gap:

IT development needs any replica QA/test environments rapidly provisioned to meet the high demand of various projects running in parallel. However, as there always is a lead time to acquire hardware, provision the OS, and install various software components, a gap exists between what IT development requests and what IT operations can realistically deliver within their budget constraints.

Costly Horizontal and Vertical Scalability:

The classical scenario is that even following due diligence testing by IT and QA staff, after an application goes into production, the IT operations team often finds itself combating a slew of performance problems. In firefighting mode, IT development often requests that more compute resources be made available by adding more CPU and RAM (vertical scalability), and by asking for more traditional servers to be added (horizontal scalability). This takes days and sometimes weeks to provision, and it places a significant strain on IT operations resources, often negatively affecting enterprise Java applications uptime.

Architectural Decision Ownership are Scattered:
Enterprise Java applications are multi-tiered, and often architectural decisions are not owned by any one stakeholder. This, in turn, slows down the rate at which the architecture matures and the implementation of key improvements.

Competing Agendas:
Each tier is dominated by a different vendor, with each driving contending agendas.

2.4 Common Products and Key Stakeholders for Enterprise Java Application Tiers

It is important to understand who the various players are in each tier, and how to positively influence the migration of Java onto vSphere. In many ways vSphere is the glue between all the application layers and the underlying hardware. VMware's vSphere is a common layer of interest among varied groups, such as applications, networking, storage, server teams, and operating systems teams.

Tier of the Java Enterprise/Web	Vendor Products & IT Stakeholders
Web Servers	**Microsoft IIS:** This is not as common as Apache because of security concerns, but Microsoft IIS does virtualize well. **Open Source Apache:** This is the predominant workhorse behind the world's most popular Web sites. These are Linux-based, and Linux administrators typically support virtualization. Linux and/or Windows Server team would have the most influence on choice of technology here
Java Server (Java Application server)	**Oracle Bea Weblogic:** Perhaps the most compelling value proposition of this technology is the highly tuned jRockit JVM. The gap between Sun's JVM (HotSpot JVM) and that of jRockit was wide five years ago, but now it is a most nonexistent. It doesn't matter which JVM is used with vSphere, as they are all equally Virtualizable. **IBM WebSphere:** The licensing model is more favourable and lowers customer costs when on vSphere, but WebSphere continues to pose challenges with TCO, administration, ease of installation, and complexity. **JBoss:** This is also complex and provides more features than you really need due to EJB implementation.

Tier of the Java Enterprise/Web	Vendor Products & IT Stakeholders
	Tomcat: This is a great alternative, but if you require production support vFabric tc Server is a better alternative. Application development architects/enterprise architects have the most influence on the choice of application server
	Note All of these Java application servers are equally Virtualizable and have been proven in production on vSphere by many VMware customers.
Load Balancers	This is a great new area. Look for F5 and Zeus for their VMware vSphere version of their load balancers. Many VMware customers are saving on additional hardware load balancer costs by purchasing the virtualized version
	Load balancer choice is typically made by the network architects

2.5 Key Benefits of Running Enterprise Java on VMware

VMware vSphere meets the challenges of Java applications with the following key benefits:

- Improved server consolidation
- Operational efficiency
- Higher availability with less complexity
- Improved Java developer productivity through VMware vFabric

The following sections discuss each benefit in more detail.

2.5.1 Improved Server Consolidation

Use All Your Server Processor Cores:
Large multi-core servers are becoming the norm, but most applications cannot take advantage of all the processor cores in a physical server. Although vSphere virtual machines can scale to 8-vCPU in vSphere 4.1 (in vSphere 5 the configuration maximum for a VM will be 32vCPU and 1TB of RAM) - if needed for the workload, it is best to adhere to smaller virtual machines as they offer placement flexibility and can help increase consolidation ratios and improve performance. Often you will find that 2-vCPU VMs are a particularly good starting point for most enterprise class Java applications.

Gain Improved Scalability:
Scalability is improved through the ability to dynamically right-size to meet traffic demands. When a particular demand subsides, you can reallocate the compute resources wherever they are needed.

Maintain Multiple Replica Environments:
Enterprise Java applications often require many QA, test, and performance test environments, all running in parallel to meet the high demands of software-release schedules. With vSphere you can maintain several environments using less hardware than traditionally

required, create replica test environments when needed, and repurpose them with minimal effort.

2.5.2 Operational Efficiency

Employ Right-size Provisioning:

Design for today's workload rather than guessing about tomorrow's. Using vSphere for an enterprise Java application deployment avoids costly over-provisioning of Java-application-server computing resources. Organizations can size their infrastructure based on current requirements and use excess capacity on their ESX hosts to run other virtual machine workloads. CPU and RAM resources can be monitored and fine-tuned at any time to meet changing performance requirements. The ability to adjust resources in this manner provides new levels of flexibility for Java application servers deployed on virtual machines, running on a vSphere platform, that are not possible without virtualization.

Improve Uptime through Seamless Software Upgrades:

VMware vMotion™ technology enables you to upgrade software on virtual machines without any loss of service or impact to uptime service-level agreements (SLAs). With vMotion you can achieve seamless software upgrades (zero downtime) and application deployments.

Create Rapid and Template-based Provisioning:

Build enterprise Java application servers with virtual machine templates. Virtual-machine templates can speed deployment times by eliminating repetitive OS installation and patching tasks. New virtual machines can have their core configuration deployed in a matter of minutes, allowing rapid provisioning of applications into production and reduction of manual work required during their deployment.

Quickly Create Test Environments:

vSphere reduces the hardware and operational costs of maintaining a Java-application test environment. This vastly accelerates delivery of enterprise Java applications due to the ease with which test and QA environments can be made available for functional and performance testing. Provisioning that used to take hours takes only minutes with vSphere. Being able to create environments from templates and cloned production copies enables you to quickly get test results for your typical enterprise Java application.

Apply to Any Major Application Server:
We have seen many production-use cases of IBM WebSphere, Oracle Weblogic, JBoss, Tomcat, and vFabric tc Server run very well on vSphere.

2.5.3 Higher Availability with Less Complexity

Reduce Planned Downtime Due to Hardware or BIOS Updates with VMware vMotion:
Virtual machines decouple the operating system and applications from the underlying hardware, allowing supporting infrastructure to grow and change rapidly. vMotion allows any virtual machine to be migrated across physical servers, even servers from different vendors with different hardware configurations. Planned downtime can be minimized. A more flexible infrastructure makes the enterprise Java application environment more resilient. In an environment without virtualization, this level of flexibility does not exist. You can also further leverage this flexibility to deploy new releases of the enterprise Java application with zero downtime.

Reduce Unplanned Downtime Due to Hardware Failure or Resource Constraints:
The vSphere platform can be leveraged to provide a wide range of availability options. VMware HA provides protection from server-hardware failure that is independent of the operating system or applications, and it works for every virtual machine running on vSphere. To aid in dynamic load balancing of Java Web-application virtual machines, VMware DRS can be used to balance workloads automatically. Solutions built on VMware HA and DRS can be deployed with minimal configuration changes and provide a robust availability

solution. These solutions can also be enhanced to provide higher levels of availability by combining them with more traditional clustering and replication options.

Implement Simple and Reliable Enterprise Java Application Disaster Recovery:

vSphere simplifies enterprise Java-application-server disaster recovery by reducing hardware-compatibility constraints and, through consolidation, the number of servers required at the DR site. Hardware independence allows the enterprise Java application-server virtual machines to be restarted on any supported ESX hosts, and server replication is simplified using virtual-machine encapsulation.

2.5.4 Improved Java Developer Productivity through VMware vFabric

VMware vSphere delivers productivity tools to IT operations, and vFabric delivers Java developer productivity tools—Spring Framework and Spring tc Server.

Developers like Spring and Tomcat for similar reasons. Both simplify the developer's job and make him or her much more productive. Spring reduces (essentially eliminates) much of the Java grunt work and Tomcat eliminates most of the time-wasting steps needed to deploy and run enterprise Java server applications.

The Spring story is about improving Java developer productivity for design, coding, test, and support. Spring is the most widely adopted Java framework and is in use by over thirty million developers. According to Evans Data, Spring accounts for over 50 percent of all deployed applications on the major Java application servers. Spring's adoption is a testimony to its productivity and power. Key architectural concepts first introduced in Spring have made their way back into the Java specification, replacing the time-consuming and cumbersome constructs of EJB.

To fully understand the synergy between the Spring Framework and tc Server, it is useful to explore the similarities and synergies of these two technologies. Spring Framework and Apache Tomcat were developed by completely separate open-source communities at different points in time, but in many ways both teams shared a common vision. Both are completely modular, carefully maintaining a lean core that can be extended when necessary. Both projects focus on developer productivity and application performance, and both have maintained their focus over a period of years, keeping the vision consistent.

2.5.4.1. Spring Leadership

- Used by three million Java developers
- Powers 50 percent of applications on IBM WebSphere, Oracle WebLogic, and Apache Tomcat
- Used by 83 percent of organizations with large development teams
- In Figure 3, the percentage of Spring framework deployments versus the top 3 application servers used in the market are shown.

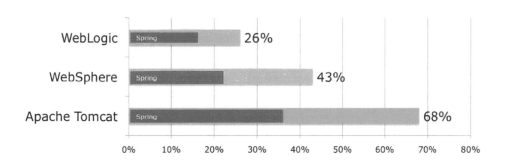

Java Application Server Usage, Source: 2008 Evans Data Survey

Figure 3: *Shows Java application server versus usage percentage including Spring Framework usage*

2.5.4.2. Emerging Architecture for the Future of Java Enterprise Application on vFabric and vSphere

The following figure (Figure 4) shows how VMware vFabric provides a robust set of features that a typical developer or application architect wants on his or her platform. VMware vFabric features such as dynamic configuration, inventory of objects, in-memory SQL, messaging service, elastic data fabric, and monitoring. This, combined with vSphere scalability, provides a solid foundation for enterprise Java applications that require an elastic application runtime.

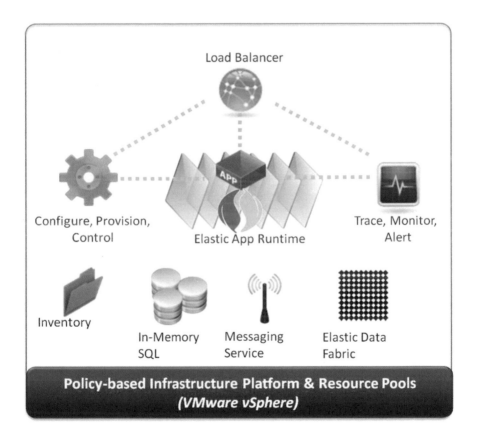

Figure 4: *Shows a high-level abstraction of the enterprise challenges that Spring vFabric suite solves*

2.5.4.3. VMware vFabric and vSphere features

Technology Layer	Feature
vSphere	Reference: http://www.vmware.com/files/pdf/key_features_vsphere.pdf
vFabric Spring framework	The vFabric Spring Framework comprises several modules that provide a range of services: **Inversion of control container (IOC)**—allows configuration of application components and lifecycle management of Java objects **Aspect-oriented programming**—enables implementation of cross-cutting routines **Data access**—works with relational database-management systems on the Java platform using JDBC and object-relational mapping tools **Transaction management**—unifies several transaction management APIs and coordinates transactions for Java objects **Model-view controller**—is a HTTP and servlet-based framework providing hooks for extension and customization **Remote-access framework**—allows configurative RPC-style export and import of Java objects over networks supporting RMI, CORBA and HTTP-based protocols including web services (SOAP) **Convention-over-configuration**—creates a rapid application-development solution for Spring-based enterprise applications in the Spring Roo module

Technology Layer	Feature
	Batch processing—provides a framework for high-volume processing featuring reusable functions including logging/tracing, transaction management, job-processing statistics, job restart, skip, and resource management
	Authentication and authorization—allows configurable security processes that support a range of standards, protocols, tools, and practices via the Spring Security sub-project (formerly Acegi Security System for Spring).
	Remote management—allows configurative exposure and management of Java objects for local or remote configuration via JMX
	Messaging—allows configurative registration of message listener objects for transparent message consumption from message queues via JMS, and improvement of message sending over standard JMS APIs
	Testing—creates support classes for writing unit tests and integration tests

Technology Layer	Feature
GemFire	GemFire is an in-memory distributed data-management platform that pools memory (and CPU, network, and optionally local disk) across multiple processes to manage application objects and behavior. Using dynamic replication and data-partitioning techniques, GemFire Enterprise offers continuous availability, high performance, and linear scalability for data-intensive applications without compromising on data consistency, even under failure conditions. In addition to being a distributed data container, it is an active data-management system that uses an optimized low-latency distribution layer for reliable asynchronous event notifications and guaranteed message delivery.
RabbitMQ	RabbitMQ is a complete and highly reliable enterprise messaging system based on the emerging AMQP standard. It is licensed under the open source and has a platform-neutral distribution, plus platform-specific packages and bundles for easy installation.
tc Server	tc Server is an enhanced version of Tomcat that is enterprise class, providing better security, deployment flexibility, and manageability to environments that have more than one hundred Java-application-server instances where complexity and manageability are a cost concern.
Hyperic	Hyperic monitors and manages every element of your web and enterprise application infrastructure, with top-down visibility into the performance of web apps regardless of location (the datacenter, a virtual environment, or the cloud).

2.6 Common Application Architecture Concerns that Can Be Resolved with VMware vFabric and vSphere

Any of the following challenges can be turned into projects that can benefit from migrations to vFabric and vSphere:

- Poor scalability in the current system
- Application downtime due to frequent software and system upgrades
- Application performance Issues
- Disaster-recovery initiatives
- Provisioning and deployment challenges
- Mergers and acquisitions (rapid business transformation)
- Migration to hosting and outsourcing
- Hardware refresh cycle
- New application development

2.7 Enterprise Java on vSphere Architecture Key Stakeholders

Understanding key stakeholders is important at each layer of the enterprise Java application world.

Load Balancer Tier (IT Operations Network Administrators): Load balancers are typically owned by the network team within the IT operations organization. A decision around the choice and function-ality of the load balancer offered is critical to the overall architecture of enterprise Java applications. Many traditional appliance/hardware-based load balancers are now offered as a VM.

Web Server Tier (IT Operations Server Administrators): This tier is often made up of Apache and in some cases IIS Web servers. Almost always the key decision makers are IT operations—you often find an advanced acceptance of vSphere in this community. The key trigger is that this is the easiest layer to virtualize and often the easiest entry point, particularly in the Apache case because they run on a Linux OS, and their administrators are already embracing virtualization.

Application Server Tier (IT Apps/Development Directors): The application-server choice is often owned by development directors. They dictate which Java application server to use, and though IT operations increasingly makes the decision with the introduction of vSphere, there may be pushback if the application development team claims the Java application server is not supported on vSphere.

Database Server Tier: The database server tier is typically split in responsibility between the application development and operations teams. It forms a critical part of enterprise Java applications architecture, as most enterprise Java applications have a RDBMS servicing their data-access needs.

NOTE:

- By adopting a flexible computing architecture such as vSphere, the IT operations team can rapidly provision and use vSphere standard HA, DRS, FT, and disaster recovery to reduce the complexity of the features used in the application servers. As a result, IT operations are more inclined to take on the management of the application server and eventually manage the full lifecycle, including upgrades, deployments, and tuning as needed.
- By having IT operations assume management of the Java application server, the IT development team can focus more on the actual business logic behind the application, as opposed to worrying about whether it will scale, and so on.

Figure 5, the relationship between which organization manages which tier is shown, while there are technology complexities associated with each of the tiers, there are certainly many logistical concerns that have to be managed due to the fact that each tier is administered by a separate organization. It is good to note, that traditional communication barriers quickly start to dissolve when Virtualizing these tiers as teams get a new perspective on solving some of the infrastructure scalability problems.

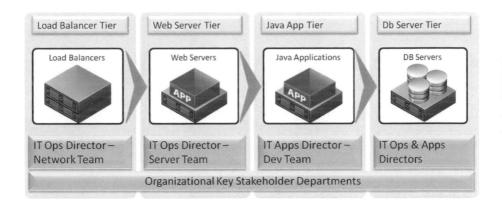

Figure 5: *Shows conventional enterprise Java applications tiers and teams that typically manage them*

2.8 Challenges Versus vSphere Benefit Matrix

2.8.1 vSphere On-demand Provisioning

Figure 6 is a vSphere diagram that shows multiple layers of flexibility and resource expansion, such as Capacity On demand, Dynamic Features (load balancing), and High Availability. In Table 1 the key infrastructure challenges versus vSphere benefits are shown.

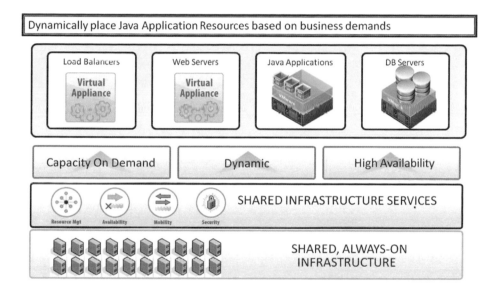

Figure 6: *Shows how vSphere adds key flexibility features to Enterprise Java Platforms*

Table 1 – *Infrastructure Challenges versus vSphere Benefits*

Infrastructure Challenges	vSphere Benefits
Hardware is rigid	Create flexible layers of expansion
Workloads are tied to physical hardware and are difficult to move or change	Quickly adapt to new or changing workloads with no user impact
New server provisioning is time-intensive	Provision new enterprise Java application-server virtual machines in minutes
Massive changes (for example, mergers) require complex project effort	Eliminate complex upgrade projects; add new resources on the fly
High availability is costly and complex	Achieve superior HA with VMware DRS
Application-server clusters are proprietary, complex, and expensive Organizational challenges exist due to the various hardware dependencies	Achieve Horizontal scalability with vSphere to achieve your SLA

2.9 Mitigation of Over-provisioning of Compute Resources with vSphere

Because traffic demand can vary immensely dependent on the popularity of the enterprise Java application being deployed, it becomes difficult for the IT development organization to set the right requirements with IT operations. In turn, IT operations often have to over-provision to accommodate for the worst possible scenario.

VMware vSphere offers many flexibility mechanisms of being able to provision compute resources on demand and when the demand subsides, you can either turn-off or re-allocate the VMs elsewhere.

2.10 Mitigation of Slow Acquisition and Deployment of Compute Resources with vSphere

Enterprise Java applications built on conventional hardware architecture are always difficult to change, as all the layers have a tight hardware dependency. A change in any one of the tiers often results in a ripple effect change to the other tiers.

Understanding how the VMware customer keeps track of change management, service delivery, and application deployments are key to enterprise Java environments. Often, you will find these responsibilities are fragmented among various departments in IT operations and IT development. It is recommend to capture each role and responsibility of personnel who do the application deployment, and find out who approves and manages the change requests. With VMware vSphere and vFabric the full lifecycle of a Java-application delivery process is available.

2.11 Use vSphere to Minimize Software Upgrades Downtime

When an operating system is running on conventional hardware, changes often cannot be done in isolation. Also, because there is no ability to incrementally release software to each server instance without affecting the application uptime, a great challenge is posed for meeting the increasing demands of the evolving Web.

In enterprise Java applications, uptime is directly linked to revenue, and showing the customer how seamless upgrades and releases can be achieved with vSphere vMotion is critical to the uptime calculation. Showing the potential revenue/SLA difference of the new uptime numbers versus the old uptime numbers becomes a strategic business initiative to roll out vSphere.

2.12 Reduce Expectation Gap

Often, IT development wants to have replica QA/test environments quickly provisioned to meet the high demand of various projects running in parallel. However, as there always is a lead time to acquire hardware, provision the OS, and install the various software components, a gap exists between what IT development requests and what IT operations can realistically deliver within its budget constraints.

VMware narrows the expectation gap between IT organization departments. Groups that were traditionally siloed are beginning to understand each other's requirements. Advocacy for virtualization almost always starts with the IT operations team, which pushes it to optimize operations. On the other hand, the IT development team becomes really interested when you tell them about how quickly lab-like replica environments can be created, and how easily multiple sandbox environments for developers and QA organizations can be deployed in matter of minutes.

2.13 Use vSphere to Reduce Cost of Horizontal and Vertical Scalability

The classic scenario is that even following due diligence testing by IT and QA staff, after an application goes into production, the IT operations team often finds itself combating a slew of performance problems. In firefighting mode, IT development often requests that more compute resources be made available by adding more CPU and RAM (vertical scalability), and by asking for more traditional servers to be added (horizontal scalability). This takes days and sometimes weeks to provision, and it places a significant strain on IT operations resources, often negatively affecting enterprise Java applications uptime.

Over the last ten years, Java-application-server vendors (Weblogic, WebSphere, JBoss, and others) saw an opportunity to solve every problem that development and operations teams had with scalability. The vendors provided IT shops with various clustering technologies that further locked them into one vendor—a solution monolith. With

VMware vSphere a new perspective is taken on scalability. VMware vSphere provides superior scalability—both vertical and horizontal scalability are easily achieved.

2.14 Building a Common Architecture with vSphere

Enterprise Java applications are multitier, and often you find that architectural decisions are not owned by one stakeholder. This in turn slows down the evolution of the architecture and any key improvements. The problem of scattered architectural decision process is particularly more prevalent with conventional hardware setup, as opposed to a virtualized platform. In a Virtualized platform, Virtualization is the common layer that binds all tiers of the Java platform together under an overall architecture, and hence architects from different tiers are constantly communicating and breaking down traditional barriers to learn more profound ways of dealing with scalability and availability requirements using Virtualization.

2.15 Common Objections and Rebuttals

"Enterprise Java applications and application servers are too business-critical to take the risk of running them in a virtualized environment."

- VMware was listed by Redmond magazine as the most reliable platform for enterprise applications. The IBM mainframe was second. VMware infrastructure has been tested across one hundred thousand customers for over a decade. Over 85 percent of VMware customers deploy VMware in production, and 46 percent of our customers have standardized on VMware vSphere as the de facto IT platform on which to deploy applications.
- In Figure 7 it is shown that approximately 41 percent of Oracle Middleware and 50% of IBM WebSphere are virtualized. This is in accordance with a VMware customer survey conducted in September 2008 across 1038 customers. No doubt much has

changed and improved since this survey particularly with vast improvements to performance in vSphere 4, and if this survey were to be re-run one would find the virtualized enterprise Java application percentage to be much higher than shown here.

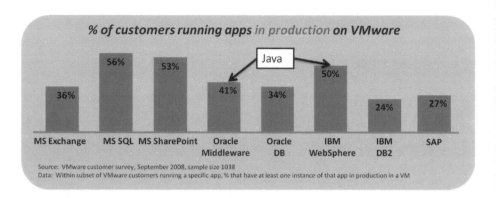

Figure 7: *Shows percentage of VMware virtualized Java deployments versus other tier-one applications*

"I'm afraid that performance will suffer if I virtualize the enterprise Java application."

It has been demonstrated many times that the performance of running Java applications in native mode versus running on vSphere is comparable. Performance does not suffer. See the Enterprise Java Application on VMware—Best Practices Guide at http://www.vmware. com/resources/techresources/1087.

In addition the best practices guide, Figure 8, a performance study is shown that was conducted by HP using an EJB based DayTrader application deployed on both physical and virtualized IBM Web-Sphere application server for a side-by-side comparison. The chart quickly shows very good performance of virtualized IBM WebSphere application server when compared with the physical case, and with a particular optimal VM configuration of two and four vCPUs. The full study can be referenced here: ***http://www.vmware.com/resources/ techresources/10095***

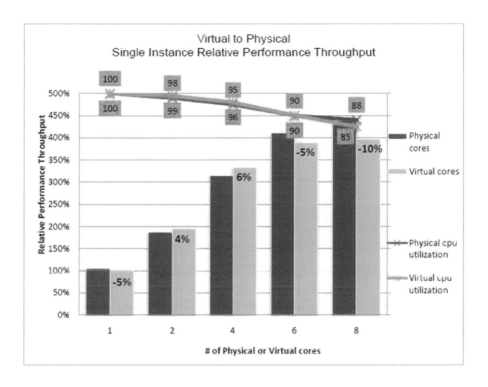

Figure 8: *Shows a performance graph throughput versus number of CPUs or vCPU conducted by HP*

"I looked at virtualization, and in my environment I can only get a three-to-one server-consolidation ratio, so I don't think it's worth it."

Consolidation is only one of the many benefits of virtualization. Many VMware customers use virtualization to perform faster, more confident upgrades, maximize application service levels, and improve manageability and recoverability.

"Where can I get support?"

See VMware support: http://www.vmware.com/support/. Or contact your application server vendor.

2.16 Licensing

IBM has favourable licensing for WebSphere on VMware (pay for what you use). For details on how IBM calculates using the ILMT tool refer to http://www-01.ibm.com/software/tivoli/products/license-metric-tool/.

Oracle requires a license for each CPU on the host (physical). If this is the case VMware, vSphere allows you to use server/host affinity to pin down all the VMs to one physical server in order to reduce licensing cost. Obviously, a HA assessment must be conducted in order to ensure there are multiple redundant copies of the application server.

Chapter 3

Enterprise Java Applications on VMware

3.1 Introduction

Enterprise Java application requirements for dynamic scalability, rapid provisioning, and high availability are growing concerns for development and operations groups today. Achieving these requirements with platforms that are completely based on conventional hardware is complex and expensive.

Virtualization is a breakthrough technology that alleviates the pressures that common enterprise Java applications requirements may impose on an organization. Features such as horizontal scalability, vertical scalability, rapid provisioning, enhanced high availability, and business continuance are some of the key attributes that are available with the VMware vSphere™ suite.

VMware vSphere, combined with the vFabric suite, provides the full breadth and depth of features to address the concerns of the developer, the deployment staff, and the datacenter administrator. These are key features in shaping the journey into the cloud.

This chapter details various use cases that directly apply to a virtualized enterprise Java application platform that provides benefits such as the following:

- Enhanced scalability
- Optimal high availability
- Business continuity
- Enhanced multitier manageability
- Full development lifecycle with VMware vFabric

3.2 Enterprise Java Application on vSphere Overview

The architecture illustrated in the following (Figure 9) shows all layers of typical enterprise Java application tiers fully virtualized to attain the benefits of a platform that provides capacity on demand, dynamic scaling, and enhanced high-availability features built in from the ground up.

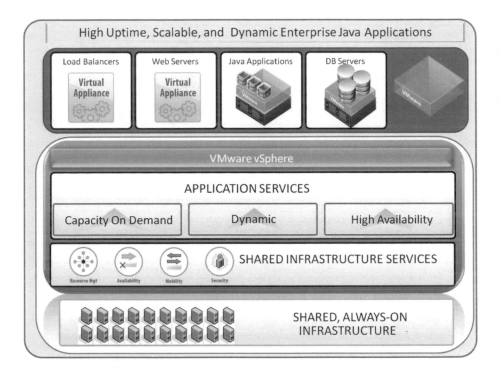

Figure 9: *Shows all of the enterprise Java tiers virtualized with VMware vSphere*

3.3 Enterprise Java Application Use Cases on vSphere

3.3.1 Enhanced Scalability

Use Case	vSphere Feature
Vertical Scalability	Virtual Machines (VMs) built on vSphere have the ability to dynamically change memory allocation and virtual CPUs at runtime. Being able to dynamically expand to accommodate for traffic bursts and to do so without compromising service levels, is a key feature. Max of 8-vCPU on each VM. While the most typical and common VM sizing is 2-vCPU and 4 vCPU for Java applications, vSphere provides the ability to build 8-vCPU VMs. In some cases, where licensing costs for additional guest OS is prohibitive and negatively affects the TCO calculation, you can choose to vertically stack your Java applications on larger VMs with up to 8-vCPUs Max memory of 255GB on an 8-vCPU VM in vSphere 4.1 (NOTE: in vSphere 5 max limits will be 32vCPU and 1TB of RAM per VM)
Horizontal Scalability	Using vSphere vCenter you can rapidly create new VMs and have them service traffic to meet your demands. Additionally, you can create VMs from predefined templates that save time and help you conform to deployment standards.

Use Case	vSphere Feature
Dynamic Scalability	Using DRS you can set up rules to help manage your SLA requirements by pooling your CPU and memory resources into clusters, and allocate and de-allocate resources based on rules you set up. DRS has the ability to automatically make recommendations that enhance availability across the cluster. For example, you can perform the following: ○ Balance average CPU loads or reservations ○ Balance average memory loads or reservations ○ Satisfy resource pool reservations For more information about vSphere DRS, see http://www.vmware.com/pdf/vsphere4/r40/vsp_40_resource_mgmt.pdf

3.3.2 Optimal High Availability

The ability to dynamically adjust resources to overcome resource constraints is paramount to achieving high availability. VMware vSphere provides more efficient management of CPU and memory resources, and minimizes downtime associated with host failure through the use of pooled clusters.

Guard Against Host Failure	When a host failure occurs, VMware HA can relocate a Java application server to another host that is active, thus minimizing downtime and disruption to service levels. This works particularly well when the Java application is part of a pooled set of instances behind a load balancer (hence maintaining the overall SLA).
What If a VM Runs Out of CPU and Memory?	You can manage CPU utilization and memory consumption within a pool of VMs by having DRS manage the total availability of these resources across the cluster. In some cases, if permitted by your hardware or OS, you gain the ability to hot add CPU and memory to a VM.
Minimize Scheduled Maintenance Downtime	You can use VMware vMotion™ to set up your hardware and software upgrades by moving VMs elsewhere while upgrading the underlying host, and/or a particular VM configuration and software deployment.

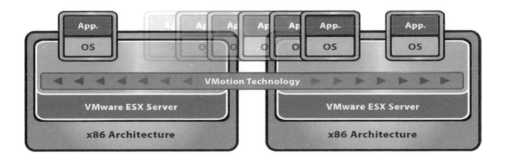

Figure 10: *Shows VMware VMotion moving VMs from one ESX host to another without downtime.*

3.3.3 Business Continuity

Use Case	vSphere Feature
Datacenter Power Outage and/ or a Natural Disaster.	• SRM allows you to execute a script that you have predefined with the recovery steps. • Create and manage recovery plans directly from the VMware vCenter server. • Discover and display virtual machines protected by storage replication using integrations certified by storage vendors.
(SRM will execute to recover all Java application services tier by tier to a predefined secondary production site)	• Extend recovery plans with custom scripts. • Monitor availability of remote site and alert users of possible site failures. • Store, view, and export results of test and failover execution from VMware vCenter server. • Control access to recovery plans with granular role-based access controls. • Leverage iSCSI, Fibre Channel, or NFS-based storage-replication solutions. • Recover multiple sites to a single shared recovery site. • Simulate and test the recovery plan • Provide a powerful API for further scripting (http://www.vmware.com/support/developer/srm-api/srm_10_api.pdf)

Figure 11 Shows SRM in action executing Business Continuity Plan (BCP) established by IT Operations earlier to failover from one site to another.

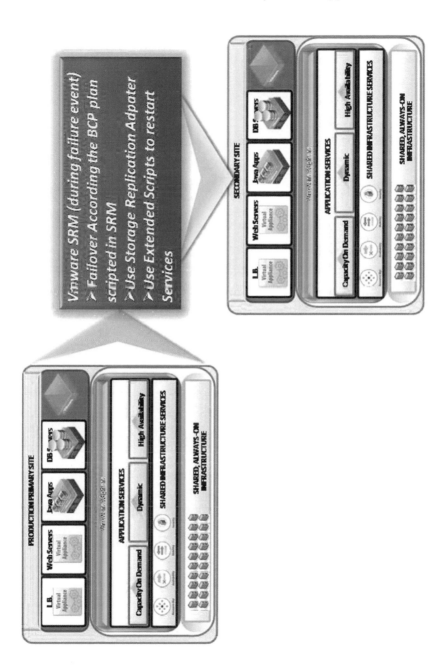

Figure 11: *Shows SRM in action between two different datacenter locations.*

3.3.4 Enhanced Multitier Manageability

Shown in Figure 12 are all of the enterprise Java application tiers virtualized with VMware vSphere which in turn offers the following enhanced manageability features:

Use Case	vSphere Feature
Management of Multitier Applications	Having load balancer, Web Server, Java Server, and DB Servers all virtualized creates a refined and easier to manage end-to-end operational model.
Define Separate Roles and Responsibilities for Operators	VMware vCenter allows you to create separate roles for application deployment administrators, developers, and super-administrators.
Rapid Provisioning	Through the use of VM templates you can quickly provision new VMs with just a few clicks in vCenter.
Cost Reduction	Having the ability to manage all VMs from one vCenter indirectly helps assist with server containment and prevents server sprawl. This saves on licensing, management costs, and power consumption. • **Enhanced Server Consolidation:** Due to the ability of virtualization to pool both CPU and memory resources you are able to achieve higher consolidation ratios and therefore significant cost savings.

- **Forecast Capacity Growth:** VMware vCenter CapacityIQ™ is a capacity-management solution for VMware vSphere. It enables users to analyze, forecast, and plan the capacity needs of their virtual datacenter environment.
- **Efficient Power Consumption with DPM:** Reduce energy consumption in the datacenter by using Distributed Power Management to consolidate workloads onto fewer servers during non-peak time, and power off idle servers when they are not needed by virtual machines in the cluster. When resource requirements of virtual machines increase, DPM brings hosts back online so service-level agreements can be met.

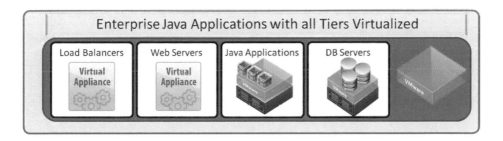

Figure 12: *Shows that all tiers of enterprise Java applications that are virtualized will benefit from maximum ROI, maintenance cost savings, power savings, and better SLAs*

3.3.5 Full Development Lifecycle with VMware vFabric

Use Case	Spring Feature
Powerful End-to-end Framework for Java Development	The VMware vFabric suite of technologies provides features that address all aspects of end-to-end development and deployment of highly flexible enterprise Java applications.

- **Inversion of control container:** configuration of application components and lifecycle management of Java objects
- **Aspect-oriented programming:** implementation of cross-cutting routines
- **Data access:** implementation of relational database management systems on the Java platform using JDBC and object-relational mapping tools
- **Transaction management:** unification of several transaction management APIs and coordinates transactions for Java objects
- **Model-view-controller:** a HTTP and servlet-based framework providing hooks for extension and customization
- **Remote access framework:** configuration of RPC-style export and import of Java objects over networks supporting RMI, CORBA and HTTP-based protocols including Web services (SOAP)
- **Convention-over-configuration:** a rapid application-development solution for Spring-based enterprise applications is offered in the Spring Roo module

	• **Batch processing**: a framework for high-volume processing featuring reusable functions including logging/tracing, transaction management, job-processing statistics, job restart, skip, and resource management • **Authentication and authorization**: a configurable security process that supports a range of standards, protocols, tools, and practices via Spring Security • **Remote management**: configure management of Java objects for local or remote configuration via JMX • **Messaging**: a configurative registration of message listener objects for transparent message consumption from message queues via JMS, improvement of message sending over standard JMS APIs • **Testing**: support classes for writing unit tests and integration tests
Distributed Caching	**GemFire** is an in-memory distributed data-management platform that pools memory (and CPU, network, and optionally local disk) across multiple processes to manage application objects and behavior. Using dynamic replication and data-partitioning techniques, GemFire Enterprise offers continuous availability, high performance, and linear scalability for data-intensive applications without compromising on data consistency, even under failure conditions. In addition to being a distributed data container, it is an active data-management system that uses an optimized low-latency distribution layer for reliable asynchronous event notifications and guaranteed message delivery.

Use Case	Spring Feature
Messaging	**RabbitMQ** is a complete and highly reliable enterprise-messaging system based on the emerging AMQP standard. It is licensed under open source and has a platform-neutral distribution, plus platform-specific packages and bundles for easy installation.
Java Runtime Container	**tc Server** is an enhanced, enterprise-class version of Tomcat that is providing better security, deployment flexibility, and manageability to environments that have more than one hundred Java application server instances, where complexity and manageability are a cost concern
Monitoring and Management	**Hyperic** monitors and manages every element of your Web and enterprise-application infrastructure, with top-down visibility into the performance of Web applications regardless of location, whether it be the datacenter, a virtual environment, or the cloud.

Build — Spring, Grails Tool Suite — Application Frameworks and Tools → Run — tc Server — Lightweight Application Runtime → Manage — Hyperic — Application Monitoring and Management

3.4 Conclusion

This chapter presented use cases that are geared to managing today's enterprise Java applications in an environment that increasingly demands higher dynamic scalability, enhanced performance, and reduced TCO. By Virtualizing each tier of the enterprise Java application platform, you are tooling your organization with the best approach to managing your environment.

By Virtualizing your enterprise Java applications, you pave the way for your organization to reap the benefits of the cloud. VMware has made a commitment to the infrastructure community to provide superior manageability of the datacenter. The recent acquisitions of SpringSource, vmForce, and Google Cloud initiatives align VMware product roadmap to help increase efficiency for the Java developer and datacenter operations community. As a result of these initiatives you can build, run, and manage your applications and infrastructure platform as one end-to-end cloud platform.

Figure 13 shows how starting with the Java developer community VMware is embracing the full lifecycle of Java development, while at the same giving the Java community a clear path to the cloud for developers that use the Spring framework to build light weight Java apps, and VMware vSphere in preparation for cloud deployment.

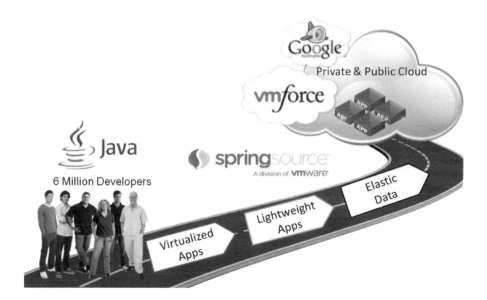

Figure 13: *Shows the evolutionary path that Java developers can follow in architecting their Java application for the cloud.*

Chapter 4

Design and Sizing of Enterprise Java on VMware

4.1 Overview

This chapter highlights key considerations and provides guidelines to IT architects who are in the process of sizing their enterprise Java applications to run on VMware vSphere™.

Our objective is to give guidance on how to obtain the best sizing configuration for your enterprise Java applications running on VMware vSphere. You are guided through the process of performance benchmarking an application, and given pointers on what to measure, what is available to be tuned, and how to best determine the optimal size for your Java application.

There is information about how to establish a benchmark and extrapolate the results to size enterprise Java applications on vSphere. However, the process by which you arrive at an accurate benchmark for virtualized applications is no different from what you would do when sizing non-virtualized Java applications. Performance-load testing and sizing practices do not differ just because you are sizing for a virtualized environment.

VMware vSphere is a flexible platform that allows vertical and horizontal scalability through various configurations, and your design and sizing should accommodate these constructs. Thorough load testing helps you establish optimal numbers for variables such as how many VMs are needed, how large VMs should be, and how many hosts and clusters are needed.

4.2 Enterprise Java Applications on VMware Architecture

As previously detailed in chapters 2 and 3, we identified the four tiers of enterprise Java application architecture as the Load Balancer Tier, Web Server Tier, Java Applications Tier, and DB Server Tier. These four tiers can be highly scalable and available if they are all virtualized. Figure 14 shows the four tiers of enterprise Java application architecture that are fully virtualized.

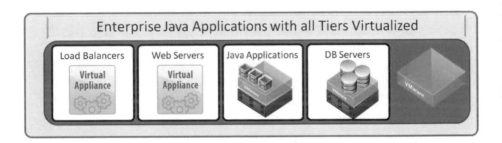

Figure 14: *Shows a scalable Java application architecture where all tiers are virtualized*

Each tier is typically separated into its own virtual machine (VM) that allows expansion both horizontally and vertically.

To size a Java application appropriately, each tier must be tuned to handle the anticipated concurrent number of users. The challenge is that each Java application architecture and runtime platform is highly customizable and has many specific properties, so it is recommended that you test your application through rigorous load testing to establish a benchmark from which you can extrapolate.

4.3 Sizing Considerations

4.3.1 Overview

As shown in Figure 15, there are three basic high-level steps when sizing.

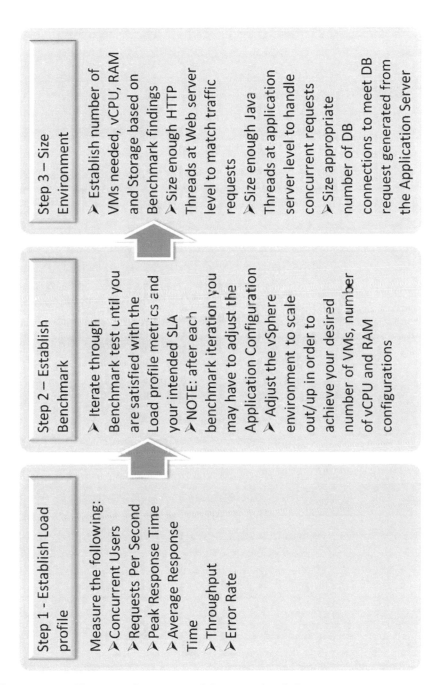

Figure 15: *Shows a three-step sizing methodology*

Step 1 - Establish Load profile

Measure the following:

- Concurrent Users
- Requests Per Second
- Peak Response Time
- Average Response Time
- Throughput
- Error Rate

Step 2 – Establish Benchmark

- Iterate through Benchmark test until you are satisfied with the Load profile metrics and your intended SLA
- NOTE: after each benchmark iteration you may have to adjust the Application Configuration
- Adjust the vSphere environment to scale out/up in order to achieve your desired number of VMs, number of vCPU and RAM configurations

Step 3 – Size Environment

- Establish number of VMs needed, vCPU, RAM and Storage based on Benchmark findings
- Size enough HTTP Threads at Web server level to match traffic requests
- Size enough Java Threads at application server level to handle concurrent requests
- Size appropriate number of DB connections to meet DB request generated from the Application Server

4.3.2 Step One: Establishing Your Current Production Load Profile

When estimating the load profile you need to measure the properties in Table 2 to establish your Java application's production load. The load profile should also have a good transactional mix of common functionality that your users execute when using the application.

Table 2: *Load Profile Properties*

Load Profile Properties	Description
Concurrent Users	Based on how you track user access to your application, you can use that information to establish peak and average user profiles. Some methods of establishing the number of users are a combination of inspecting log-in-log-out functionality, or if that doesn't exist, some user-access logs in combination with URL cookie tracking, or a commercial monitoring tool. Concurrent users is a common term to express the load applied during a test. This metric measures how many users are active at any one point in time. This is different from requests per second (RPS) because potentially one user can generate a high number of requests, while other users may generate a relatively low number. When establishing your load test, the delay between the requests is the think-time. Average think-time can vary depending on your application.

Requests Per Second (RPS)	RPS is the measurement of how many requests are being sent to the target server. It includes requests for HTML pages; CSS style sheets, XML documents, JavaScript libraries, images, and Flash/multimedia files.
	In addition to these requests, there are requests for dynamic pages, JSP and others that are server-bound requests, which are from the Web server that are handled by the application
	server. You can establish the request mix (how many static requests versus dynamic requests) by studying the redirect rules and the access logs of your Web server. Dynamic requests are important as they turn into Java threads being consumed from the Java application server. In turn, if they access the DB, then DB connections are checked out from the JDBC pool configured at the Java application server.
Average Response Times	This can be measured as the time to first and/or last byte received from your application requests. If you have response-time SLA monitoring in place, you can use reports from those tools. If not, you can establish this via benchmark during the load test.
Peak Response Time	This measures the round trip for the request/response cycle.

4.3.3 Step Two: Establish a Benchmark

This section is on establishing a benchmark, conduct vertical-scalability and horizontal-scalability tests.

In the vertical-scalability test, establish how large a VM can be and how many JVMs can be stacked on top before you reach the desired SLA and tolerable CPU saturation levels. The resulting VM configurations with the various JVMs from this test form the building-block VM for the scale-out test. If during the scale-out test you reach saturation, investigate all of the layers (network, application configuration, and vSphere) and determine where the bottleneck is. Remove the bottleneck and repeat the test by adjusting the number of VMs. Alternately, if you find that the original building-block VM has a miss-configuration at the VM and/or application-configuration level, adjust and repeat the vertical load test to determine a new building-block VM.

Use the VM from the scale-up test as a repeatable building block for the scale-out test. This helps in two ways. First, it allows for a well-defined and known configuration to be repeated, eliminating any configuration guesswork. Second, it means all of the nodes in your application cluster are symmetrical, thus simplifying load-balancer logic as a load balancer distributes load equally without needing to know the configuration of the VM. For example, if your VM is 2-vCPU, then all of the VMs in the application cluster are 2-vCPU and potentially can handle the same workload. Of course, if the VMs had different specifications, the load-balancer layer would not know about this unless you have a special load-balancer configuration to accommodate for the asymmetrical VM configurations in the application cluster. Refer to Figure 16 for an illustration on how to establish the Building Block VM and the scale out test.

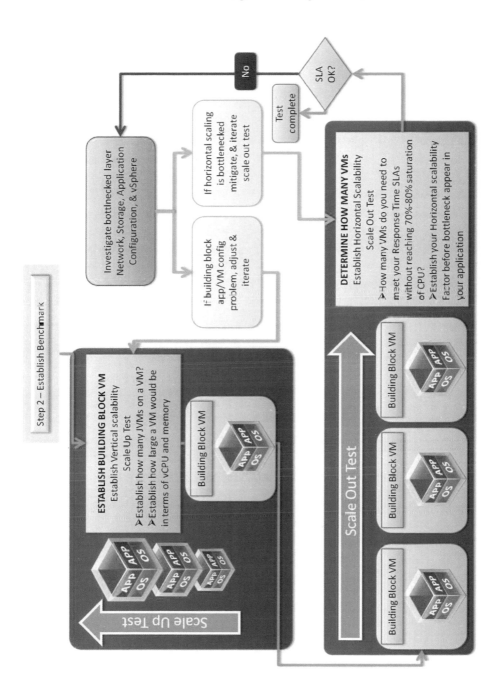

Figure 16: *Shows the benchmark workflow*

NOTE: DRS is turned off during the initial scale-Up and scale-out test, however once you have conducted load testing to a satisfactory level, you can then turn on DRS and see the effects of VMotion on your application. This could be very interesting measure for longevity testing, i.e. letting the applications run for many hours to simulate a full day of operations, and hence measure how DRS via VMotion is able to further balance the workloads across the ESX hosts.

The following table describes some key considerations when sizing the benchmarking environment.

Table 3: *Key Considerations for Sizing the Benchmark Environment*

Consideration	Description
Establish vertical scalability	This test establishes the building-block VM. This VM is used as a repeatable VM for the scale-out test. Each VM in the application cluster of the scale-out test will be based on this building-block VM. Determine the size of the VM in terms of vCPU and memory to meet the desired SLA. Establish how many JVMs can be stacked up on this VM
Establish horizontal scalability	The horizontal-scalability load test takes the building-block VM from the vertical-scalability load test and uses that to scale out the load-testing environment.

	If saturation occurs before reaching the desired SLA, investigate whether this is due to any of the network, application-layer, vSphere, or storage layers. When the desired SLA that can accommodate a production level of traffic is reached, you have reached your desired system size.
	This system is usually the production-to-be configuration as most migration to virtualization projects starts with a completely new environment and then goes through the described load testing in the baking period.
Establish appropriate thread ratios (HTTP threads: Java threads:DB connections)	This is the ratio of HTTP threads to Java threads to DB connections.
	Establish initial setup by assuming that each layer requires a 1:1:1 ratio of HTTP threads: Java threads: DB connections, and then based on the response time and throughput numbers, adjust each of these properties until you have satisfied your SLA objectives.

Consideration	Description
	Using the above example of one hundred concurrent requests, your ratio would initially be one hundred HTTP threads to one hundred Java threads to one hundred DB connections. For example, if you have one hundred HTTP requests initially submitted to the Web server, assume that all of these will have an interaction with Java threads and in turn DB connections. Of course, in reality as you perform the benchmark testing you will find that not all HTTP threads are submitted to the Java application server, and in turn not all Java application server threads will each require a DB connection. You may find your ratio for one hundred requests translates to one hundred HTTP threads: twenty-five Java threads: ten DB connections. This depends on the nature of the enterprise Java application behaviour—benchmarking helps you establish this ratio.
Establish appropriate HTTP threads for Web server	HTTP threads (Web server). Whether you are using Apache or IIS as your Web server you need to accommodate enough HTTP worker threads that can facilitate the requests per second that your application incurs.

In Apache these requests are identified by the MaxClients attribute. Refer to Apache tuning guides if you need to further tune, but most default values should be an adequate starting point. Take into account the scale-out number of Apache instances |

when sizing for MaxClients. For example, if you have one thousand concurrent requests and four apache VM nodes, then each node only needs a MaxClients value of 250. In IIS, similarly, try to set MaxConnections appropriately. Refer to the vendor documentation for settings.

HTTP threads from the Web server serve *static content and dynamic content.* Static content such as HTML and images are completely handled by your Web-server layer, and the threads that are used to service these don't affect the Java-application-server layer directly. Conversely, when a Web server detects a request for dynamic content such as a request for JSP/other, these requests are directed to the Java application server where a Java-application-server thread is checked out from the Java application server's pool to service the request. Benchmarking helps establish the total transactional mix and guides you in adjusting the thread ratios up or down accordingly.

Establish appropriate thread ratios (DB connections at the Java application JDBC pool config)	Adjust the number of available DB connections in the application server's connection pool settings, and count the number of potential Java threads that would need a DB connection. For simplicity, you can assume 1:1 ratio, and add some room to reduce potential contention or a race for DB connections.

Consideration	Description

	Deadlock can occur if the application requires more than one concurrent connection per thread, and the database connection pool is not large enough for the number of threads. Suppose that each of the application threads requires two concurrent database connections, and the number of threads is equal to the maximum connection-pool size. Deadlock can occur when both of the following are true:
	    ○ Each thread has its first database connection, and all are in use.
	    ○ Each thread is waiting for a second database connection, and none becomes available because all threads are blocked.
	
	 To prevent the deadlock in this case, increase the maximum connections value for the database connection pool by at least one. This allows at least one of the waiting threads to obtain a second database connection and avoids a deadlock scenario.
	
	 Refer to your application-server documentation for any additional JDBC pool tuning you can do in terms of start size of the connection pool min/max, growth rate, idle connections recycle, timeout parameters, and so on.

Establish JVM configuration	There are various GC algorithms that you can use. From a virtualization perspective all of the GC algorithms are equally usable and behave similarly whether on native or virtual.
	o The GC tuning that you did in the native environment is reusable as-is on Java running on vSphere.
	o Because of the ability to provide multiple vCPUs to VMs, typically the concurrent mark and sweep, CMS collector should be considered.
	The more vCPUs you have, the more improved the GC cycle in terms of being able to reduce the pauses as more CPU cycles are made available with increased vCPU.
	Using ++UseLargePages HotSpot-JVM (in IBM JVM it is -Xlp and jRockit -XXLargePages) flag and equivalent OS configuration is important.
	Set your -Xms2048m equal to -Xmx2048m. A 2GB heap space is large enough for most applications, but one size cannot fit all, and you have to experiment to determine the best fit. If you find that you have to increase vCPU consider increasing heap as well.

Consideration	Description
	Set -Xss192k. Although you can experiment to determine what is best for your environment, in some cases you might reduce this to a point where a StackOverflow occurs, in which case you have reduced it too far. Increase it to the point where the StackOverflow exception no longer occurs during the load test.
	-Xmn, new generation size, is set at 25 percent to 33 percent of the total heap size. In most cases, the default size is adequate, and letting the JVM make the selection is your best option. However, if you have to experiment with this, then setting new generation to 25 percent to 33 percent may be a good starting point for your load-testing exercise. If your application creates a large number of objects during short-lived threads like in a Web application, experiment by load testing to determine the best fit.
	For additional information refer to *Chapter 6*.

4.3.4 Step Three: Size-Production Environment

Use the environment determined in Step Two as a candidate on which to base your production system. You can use this environment because it is based on repeated iterations of horizontal and vertical scalability that have lead you to parameters that have been tested for your application's intended traffic level and SLAs.

We find that some customers turn this into a candidate staging, load-testing, and QA environment, and then build a replica production environment based on the specifications determined in Step Two.

If due to budget restrictions, only a scaled-down version of the intended new production system was benchmarked in Step Two, exercise extreme caution when making extrapolation assumptions. You must thoroughly understand the horizontal and vertical scalability ratio and be on the lookout for any bottlenecks and saturation points on your system when CPU utilization reaches 70 percent.

Because virtualization projects are typically built on a new environment (whether new or repurposed hardware), it is always advisable to follow the approach in Step Two, where you essentially create a prebaked production environment that can be turned on as turnkey environment during rollout. This greatly simplifies rollout and rollback planning.

4.4 Sizing FAQs for Enterprise Java Applications on VMware

Much of this chapter focuses on a benchmarking effort that applies for sizing Java applications, regardless of whether they are running on physical or virtualized servers. Because most virtualization projects are about driving consolidation ratios, and because VMware vSphere offers many constructs for scaling horizontally and vertically with relative ease, the following questions about design considerations are frequently asked.

"What new decisions must be made for applications running on virtual that we did not have to make for native environments?"

You have to determine the optimal size of the repeatable building-block VM. Establish this by benchmarking, along with total scale-out factor. This involves determining how many concurrent users each single vCPU configuration of your application can handle and then extrapolating that to your production traffic to determine overall compute-resource requirements such as vCPU, memory, storage, and network. Having a symmetrical building block (for example, every VM having the same number of vCPUs), helps keep load distribution from your load balancer even. The benchmarking tests help you determine how large a single VM should be (vertical scalability) and how many VMs you will need (horizontal scalability).

"I have conducted extensive GC sizing and tuning for our current enterprise Java application running on physical. Do I have to adjust any sizing when moving this Java application to a virtualized environment?"

No. All tuning that you perform for your Java application on a physical system is transferrable to your virtual environment. However, because virtualization projects are typically about driving a high consolidation ratio, it is advisable that you follow the guidelines within this chapter to establish an ideal compute-resource configuration for your individual VMs, the number of JVMs within a VM, and the overall number of VMs on the ESX host.

There are several caveats. For example, if you are switching from a 32-bit to a 64-bit JVM, revisit your tuning parameters. Often 64-bit JVMs, due to their increased requirement for address pointer allocation of certain types, require that you adjust your JVM heap memory higher by as much 30 percent to 50 percent. You need to test to verify this. Refer to Chapter 7 for further details.

When migrating from a physical server that is only 5 percent to 15 percent CPU-utilized to a virtualized server (ESX host) that is 70 percent utilized, there may be a need to revisit your tuning parameters, as Java application issues that are dormant on an underutilized server may surface when you drive the CPU utilization to 70 percent and beyond.

"How many and what size of virtual machines will I need?"

This depends on the nature of your application. We most often see 2-vCPU VMs as a common building block for Java applications. One of the guidelines is to tune your system for more scale out as opposed to scale up. This is not an inflexible rule as it depends on your organization's architectural best practices. Smaller, more scaled-out VMs may provide better overall architecture, but you incur the additional guest OS licensing costs. If this is a constraint then you can tune towards larger 4-vCPU VMs and stack more JVMs on it. For tier-1 enterprise class Java applications always start with a one JVM to one 2vCPU VM, and maintain this ratio of JVM to vCPU as one JVM to 2vCPU if you choose to scale up/out.

"What is the correct number of virtual machines per vSphere host?"

This depends on the nature of your enterprise Java application. On vSphere 4.1, you can have up to 320 VMs configured on an individual host.

"What is the correct number of JVMs per virtual machine?"

There is no one definitive answer as this largely depends on the nature of your application. The benchmarking you conduct can reveal the limit of the number of JVMs you can stack up on a single VM.

The more JVMs you put on a single VM, the more JVM overhead/cost is incurred when initializing a JVM. Alternately, instead of stacking up multiple JVMs within a VM, you can increase the JVM size vertically by adding more threads and heap size. This can be achieved if your JVM is within an application server such as Tomcat, so instead of increasing the number of JVMs, you can increase the number of concurrent threads available and resources that a single Tomcat JVM can service for your n-number of applications deployed and their concurrent requests per second. The limitation of how many applications you can stack up within a single application-server instance/JVM is bounded by how large you can afford your JVM heap size to be and the performance impact. A very large JVM heap size beyond 4GB needs to be tested for performance and GC cycle impact, and the trade-offs need to be examined. This concern is not specific to virtualization—it equally applies to physical-server setup.

NOTE: That if your application happens to be a very busy enterprise class application in the vicinity of 500 concurrent transactions per vCPU, it is always best to maintain a ratio of 1 JVM to 2VCPU. This will give optimal configuration by allowing the busy GC thread to concurrently execute while the other vCPU is left process user transactions. The most common configuration these days is 1 JVM on 2vCPU VM, with about 4G Heap space.

Follow the recommendations in Section 4.3, as it provides you with guidance on how to start tuning GC if you have done this exercise already.

"What effect will vMotion/DRS/HA have on my sizing if things move around?"

It is important to test the horizontal scalability of your application within a vSphere DRS cluster. A vSphere cluster can be configured with up to thirty-two vSphere host machines per cluster, 320 VMs per vSphere host, and a total of three thousand VMs per vSphere DRS cluster.

You should test your application during the benchmark for effects of vMotion on response time of the application.

When sizing and benchmarking for the individual size of the VM and JVM ratios for vCPU and memory, it is important to calculate your ratios for the entire cluster. Typically you first carry out a test in an isolated environment with DRS disabled to see how far you can push things on a single host. The second set of benchmarking tests examines the effects of a VMware DRS cluster and vMotion. In this case you need a minimum of two host machines. Experiment with measuring response times when there are vMotion events.

"For the benchmarking environment I am only budgeted for a small amount of hardware for the POC and cannot replicate all of the hardware needed to meet my production SLA. Can I use a scaled-down version of my production environment to conduct the sizing exercise and then extrapolate from that?"

A simplistic answer is no, because the scalability of your application on physical hardware and/or on vSphere varies as you increase load, and saturation occurs at some point as bottlenecks appear anywhere on the stack. It is typical to start to see saturation around 70 percent, and beyond that the scalability diverges exponentially from the linear line.

Keep in mind that even below saturation levels when scalability is assumed to be linear, it is never perfectly linear. This is why you have to test both the horizontal- and vertical-scalability ratios for your application.

Follow the recommendations in Step Two to establish your repeatable building-block VM by conducting a vertical-scalability test, and then use the building-block VM as the basis of the scale-out load-test environment by horizontally replicating it. Follow the sizing recommendations in Section 4.3 of this chapter. You can perform a very small POC on limited hardware, and then follow the benchmarking recommendations in Section 4.1.3 to build out the production-to-be environment through the iterative process of load testing and retuning and reconfiguring to meet your SLA. The final, resulting environment configuration can either be repurposed as production for go-live, or a new system based on the configuration can be built to provision the production environment.

4.5 Conclusions and Recommendations

Key takeaways:

- Conduct a benchmark test as outlined in Section 4.3 while taking into account all of the various design considerations.
- The environment configuration for application software and infrastructure that you determine in Step Two can be viewed as a prebaked production rollout-ready environment. This is a safe assumption, assuming you have simulated the full breadth and depth of the application's load profile and the complete technology stack. Because virtualization projects are typically built on a new environment (whether new or repurposed

hardware), it is always advisable to follow the approach in Step Two, where you essentially create a prebaked production environment that can be turned on as turnkey environment during rollout. This greatly simplifies rollout and rollback planning.

- Design your system towards a scale-out as opposed to scale up. Remember that your benchmark tests help you select optimal numbers. There are times where you may find it beneficial to increase heap size when you are increasing vCPU on a VM (vertically scale/scale-up).

- vSphere environments have been proven in terms of network, storage, and ESX configuration, since typically print servers and other non-critical workloads might have already been migrated. Refer to the following guides for additional information:

    o VMware vSphere Resource Management Guide: http://www.vmware.com/pdf/vsphere4/r41/vsp_41_resource_mgmt.pdf
    o VMware vCenter Server Performance and Best Practices: http://www.vmware.com/files/pdf/techpaper/vsp_41_perf_VC_Best_Practices.pdf
    o SAN Design and Deployment Guide: http://www.vmware.com/pdf/vsp_4_san_design_deploy.pdf
    o Performance Troubleshooting for vSphere: http://communities.vmware.com/docs/DOC-10352
    o vSphere Networking Best Practices: http://www.vmworld.com/docs/DOC-5122

- Use local and global balancers.
- Use vMotion and VMware DRS to manage equal load distribution among vSphere hosts.
- Use Java application cluster, and/or distributed cache if your application requires low latency, higher availability and fault tolerance, for example applications that are mission critical systems. Otherwise, you may find that using DRS and VMware HA is more than sufficient to initially meet your SLA.

Chapter 5

High-availability Designs of Enterprise Java on VMware

5.1 Overview

A number of designs are available to support high availability for enterprise applications on VMware. Enterprise Java application architecture has four main tiers, as shown in Figure 17 and in earlier chapters.

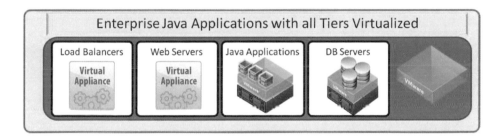

Figure 17: *Shows an enterprise Java application architecture with all tiers virtualized*

Each tier is typically separated into its own virtual machine (VM) that allows expansion both horizontally and vertically at runtime without downtime. This feature is critical to being able to deliver zero-downtime application deployments, a dynamic ability to handle traffic bursts, and a better disaster-recovery mechanism.

This chapter addresses several dimensions of the high-availability architecture of enterprise Java applications on VMware, including the following:

- Ability to perform zero-downtime (seamless) application releases during scheduled maintenance
- Ability to handle traffic bursts and maintain adequate SLAs
- Ability to perform effective disaster recovery

Key considerations and guidelines are provided for IT architects who are in the process of evaluating various high-availability options for enterprise Java applications.

5.2 Phased Approach to Achieving Higher Availability

Figure 18 illustrates the phased approach to achieving higher availability. Enterprise architects can drive the technology and the IT organization to a new SLA and maturity level as they implement each of the proposed phases.

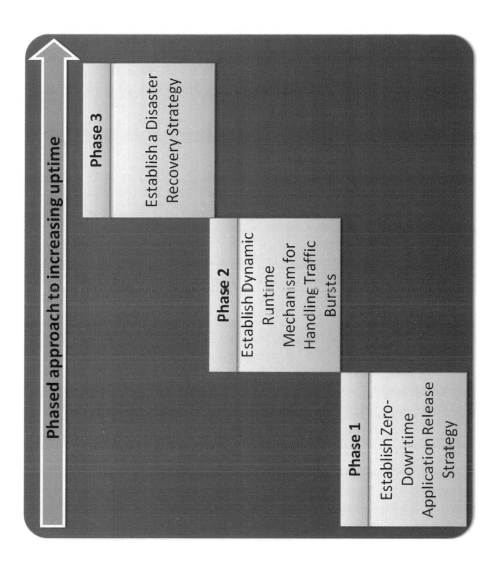

Figure 18: *Shows a phased approach to achieving higher availability*

5.3 Phase One: Establish Zero-Downtime Application-Release Strategy

5.3.1 Background

The following are key challenges when designing and implementing zero-downtime releases for enterprise Java applications:

- Eliminate manual-release steps through automation: Application deployment often takes an unnecessarily long time because of too many manual steps in the release process. The first step towards a zero-downtime design should be to fully script each action. A scripting approach that helps to gather all the steps in each tier is to use Apache Ant, along with various shell scripts, and the VMware vSphere™ API (see section 5.6 of this chapter on the VI-Java API). Fully automating all of the deployment steps helps to automate the rollback process as well. VMware provides the ability to take a snapshot of the VM's state, which is helpful if a rollback needs to be triggered.
- Determine your failover point: The most prudent method of switching is from the load-balancer layer. At the load-balancer layer you have the ability to divert traffic in a user-friendly manner with minimal impact or disruption to your application's SLA.
- Deal with synchronizing the state of the database, ultimately there needs to be two databases. One is for the primary site, and the other is for the secondary site. Synchronizing and keeping the second database up to date is critical. This is particularly true if your database schema is being altered during the release. In some cases, where the schema does not need to be changed for the release because there are only data changes, the release can be more easily accomplished without having to use multiple database instances.
- Release-orchestration challenges: Understanding the steps and dependencies of the various applications running on

various VMs is critical to formulating the release orchestration. Java applications running on VMware vSphere can benefit from VMware vMotion™ to move VMs around without downtime.

- Choose a release window: It is not an easy task to choose an appropriate release-outage window for an enterprise Java application that has a 24/7 active user base. VMware vSphere features, along with the zero-downtime release strategy, help alleviate the need to negotiate a release window. Even so, it is prudent to perform releases during off-peak hours, as the need to switch between production-1 to a scaled-down version of production-2 (see Figure 19) minimizes additional infrastructure complexity.

5.3.2 An Architecture for Zero-Downtime Application Release

Figure 19 shows two production site replicas within one datacenter. This configuration provides the ability to switch over from the production-1 application cluster to the production-2 application cluster. A high-level procedure for switching from one application cluster to another is also provided. The notion of application cluster here can be any set of VMs that make up a vertical segment of your application that is being upgraded - meaning all of the software components that make up your deployment, for example the web server, the application server, and the database server. You can also optionally capture these as vApps, where multiple VMs can be captured as a vApp. NOTE: Production-1 and Production-2 are in the same datacenter location, they just form a logical perimeter around the set of VMs that you are about to orchestrate and update.

The 5 high level zero-downtime orchestration steps for Figure 19 -

1. Before the release date, make a production replica of production-1 and name it production-2. Use VM cloning to quickly and easily create the replica.

2. Switch from production-1 to production-2 using the load balancer.
3. Take a snapshot of the VMs in the production-1 environment. Begin the application-deployment/release process using a master deployment script in section 5.6.
4. Synchronize the databases between production-1 and production-2 because more data might have been introduced during the time production-2 was live.
5. If the QA process confirms that the deployment was successful, you can switch at the load-balancer level to production-1. Otherwise, rollback to the last saved snapshot (from Step 3) and then switch back.

Because a release is typically performed during off peak hours, prodcution-2 may be a scaled down version of production-1.

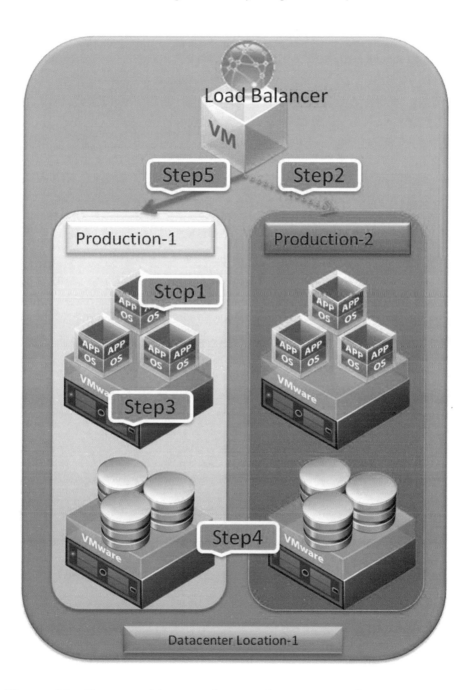

Figure 19: *Shows architecture for zero-downtime application release*

5.4 Phase Two: Establish Dynamic Runtime Mechanism to Handle Traffic Bursts

The ability to handle traffic bursts requires that you are able, at runtime and without downtime, to increase the size of VMs, add more ESX hosts to a cluster, and increase the number of VMs. Additionally, it helps if you use a load balancer that is able to integrate with the VMware API to divert traffic to newly added resources. The F5 load balancer has this capability.

In addition to being able to add resources, you can easily remove them if they are no longer needed.

5.4.1 Vertical Scalability of VMs: CPU and Memory Hot Add

VMs with guest operating systems that support hot add of CPU and memory can take advantage of this ability to change the VM configuration at runtime without any interruption to VM operations. This is particularly useful when you are trying to increase the ability of the VM to handle more traffic.

Figure 20 shows feature of being able to add new compute resource such as CPU, RAM, and Storage to the VM is shown. As illustrated, what was a small VM can be scaled up vertically with more vCPU and RAM when needed using the HotPlug features.

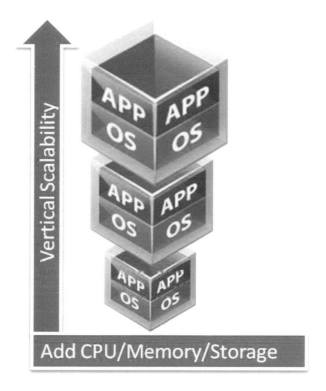

Figure 20: *Shows the ability of VMware virtual machines to scale vertically by adding compute resource*

Plan ahead and enable this feature. The VM must be turned off to enable the hot-plug feature. Once enabled, hot add of CPU and memory can be done at runtime without VM shutdown as long as the guest OS supports it. In Figure 21 the screen for enabling the hot-plug feature is shown.

To enable the hot-plug/hot-add feature, click VM > Edit Setting, and click the Options tab.

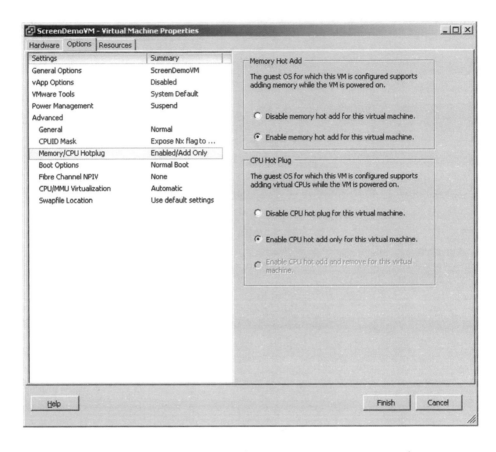

Figure 21: *Shows the virtual machine properties options tab*

To add CPU without shutting down, select CPUs, select the number of virtual processors, and click Add. (You can add memory in a similar manner.) Refer to screen shown in Figure 22.

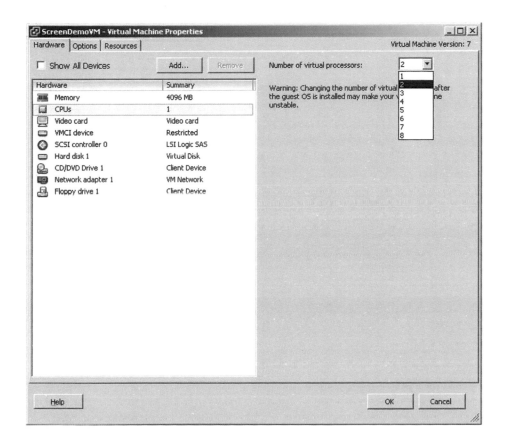

Figure 22: *Shows the virtual machine properties—adding CPUs*

Often, when there is a need to increase Java heap space, there is also a need to increase vCPU count to get the best GC cycle performance. Keep in mind that there are many other aspects to GC tuning.

Always size the guest OS at least 0.5-1GB greater than the total heap space used. If multiple JVMs are being deployed on the VM, add each JVM's max heap size to the final guest-OS memory allocation.

5.4.2 Horizontal Scalability: Add new VMs

As illustrated in Figure 23 you can create new VMs and add them to a DRS cluster, or create them on the intended host. Some load balancers such as F5 BIG-IP can detect the new VM, add it to its pool configuration, and divert traffic to it.

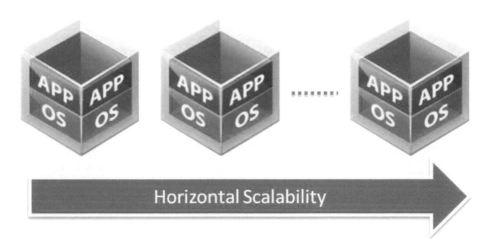

Figure 23: *Shows the ability of VMware vSphere to scale horizontally by allowing new VMs to be added*

5.4.3 Adding New Hosts to a Cluster Using DRS and Resource Pools

Various hosts that make up the tiers of a particular enterprise Java application can be grouped in a cluster, where HA can be used to restart VMs on another host in case of a host failure. You can also use DRS to balance the load between hosts in a cluster to achieve best performance. Figure 24 illustrates how you can add more hosts and then being able as a result add more VMs in order to facilitate a horizontal scale out of an application.

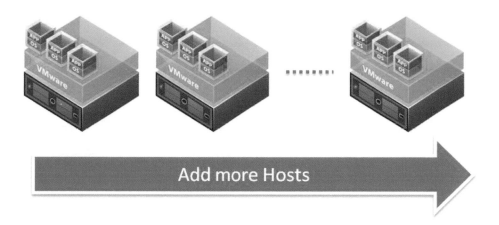

Figure 24: *Shows the ability of VMware vSphere to add new hosts to a cluster of hosts*

Multiple resource pools can be used within a cluster to manage compute-resource consumption by either reserving the needed memory for the VMs within a resource pool, or by limiting or restricting to a specified level within the pool. This feature also helps meet SLAs and quality-of-service objectives.

Figure 25 illustrates how you can enable the HA and DRS for the ESX Cluster.

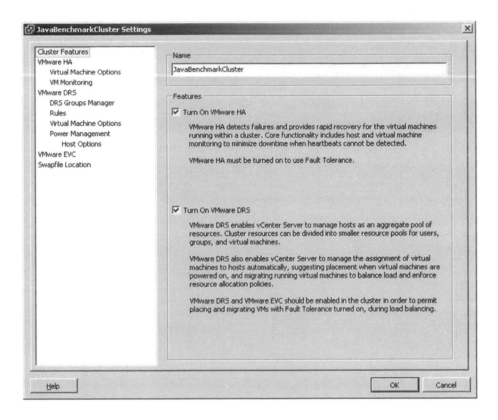

Figure 25: *Shows the screen for enabling HA and DRS*

Figure 26 shows the three available automation levels for DRS: **Manual, Partially automated**, and **Fully automated**. In most cases, administrators new to virtualization first use **Manual** mode and watch the DRS recommendations over a period of time. When satisfied that the recommendations are valid, they set it to **Fully automated**. This is especially helpful when you have large number of hosts and VMs to manage.

Further, DRS allows you to separate or couple VM rules. For example, if you have two Web servers load balancing traffic for your application, you would not want to place both of them on the same host because both would go down if the host fails. You can set up a DRS rule that both Web servers should always be on separate hosts.

Conversely, you may choose to always have two VMs on the same host if they frequently need to communicate with each other in a way that creates a lot of traffic.

With VMware HA and VMware DRS turned on, it is possible to achieve 99.9 percent uptime without the need for any additional clustering technologies. This assumes that other parts of the infrastructure have adequate redundancy and there are no performance issues within the Java-application code.

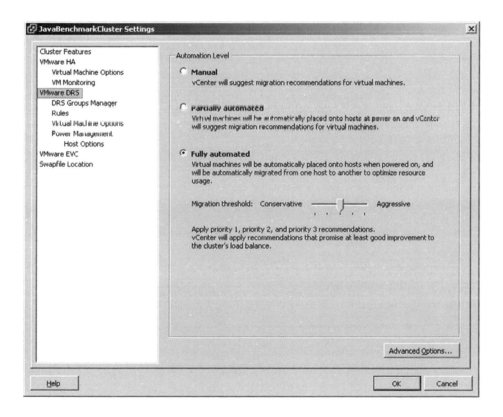

Figure 26: *Shows the screen for automation levels for DRS*

5.4.4 Using a Load Balancer to Discover Newly Added VMs

Creating new VMs in vSphere is straightforward. However, it has always been a challenge to make the necessary network changes to configure these new VMs so that a load balancer can direct traffic to them. F5 BIG-IP, through its iControl API, integrates with VMware vCenter to receive instructions that can trigger it to adjust network traffic in response to a spike in application usage. When new VMs are added in vCenter, the F5 BIG-IP Load Balancer can automatically add those new servers to its load-balancing pool and can direct traffic to them.

Figure 27 illustrates how a load balancer automatically reconfigures traffic to the load-balancing pool based on information it receives from vCenter to start directing traffic to the new VMs.

For further examples and solutions of F5 and VMware vSphere you can refer to the following: http://www.f5.com/solutions/applications/vmware/vsphere/

Here is a great example of a graceful shutdown: http://devcentral.f5.com/Tutorials/TechTips/tabid/63/articleType/ArticleView/articleId/254/iControl

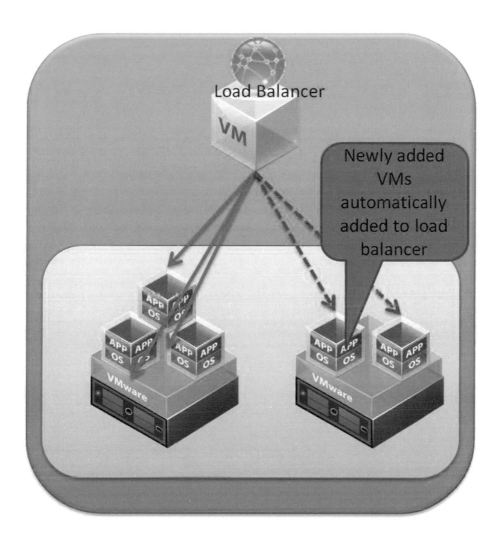

Figure 27: *Shows using a load balancer to discover newly added VMs*

5.5 Phase Three: Establish a Disaster-recovery Strategy

The integration of F5 BIG-IP Global Load Balancer and VMware SRM provides a complete solution for automated disaster recovery between two datacenters, or to the cloud. In the event of disaster, SRM can orchestrate the failover of VM guests and virtual infrastructure between the two sites, while the BIG-IP Global Load Balancer redirects all incoming client-application traffic to the secondary site. The F5 BIG-IP Global Load Balancer and SRM are easily integrated via the F5 iControl API. Refer to Figure 28 for a high level illustration of SRM between 2 sites. The key feature to make this implementation possible is to use a Storage Replication Adapter (SRA) for your particular storage device. You can find a list of SRM SRAs here: http://www. vmware.com/pdf/srm_storage_partners.pdf

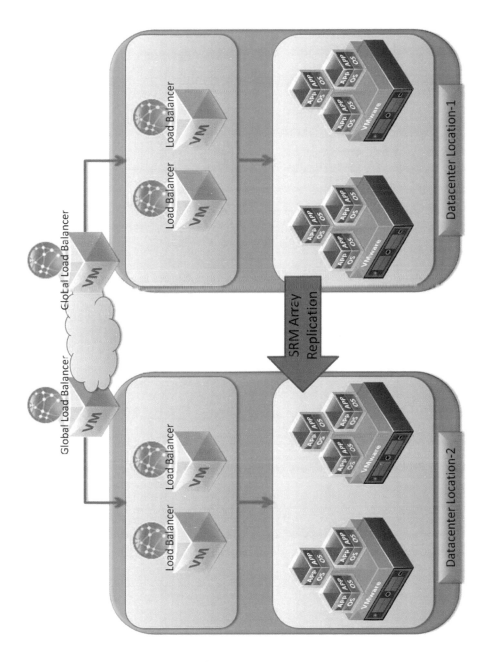

Figure 28: *Shows a typical VMware vCenter site-recovery manager setup between two sites*

5.6 Example: Master Deployment Script

This section provides information about creating a master deployment script for enterprise Java applications on VMware. The script has the ability to interact with VMs, manipulate guest-OS files, and interact with the Java application server (WAR file deployments) and the database. You can use Apache and the VMware-VI-Java-API for interaction with the VMs to create a master script for all of the deployment steps. The following discusses various key functionalities and provides the needed script snippets.

Note Though a lot of this functionality is available from the vSphere Client via a UI, it is useful to be able to script this when you have multiple VMs to deal with.

The general framework of the master deployment script involves the following functional steps:

1. Take snapshots of the VMs.
2. Interact with the load balancer to activate the switchover from one application environment to another.
3. Interact with the Java application server to deploy the application WAR file.
4. Interact with the database server to apply SQL scripts that may be part of your application release.
5. Interact with VM to revert to prior snapshots (if rollback is need).

The following script snippets are applicable for a single VM scenario. You need to modify these scripts to handle multiple VMs. To iterate for multiple VMs you can reuse the single VM methods presented here in a multiple iteration/loop through the set of VMs that are part of the environment undergoing a Java application release.

5.6.1 Brief Summary of VI Java APIs

The VI Java API has functionality to manipulate the following areas:

- Virtual Machine APIs: CloneVM,CreateVM,GetUpdates,Migrate VM,RemoveVmDisk,VMClone,VMReconfig,VMSnapshot,VmNi cOp,VmRename
- Cluster APIs: Create, Affinity rules , DRS vMotion History
- Storage APIs: AddDatastore,CopyFile,PrintStorageSystem,Que ryVirtualDisk
- Network APIs: AddDVS,AddNIC,AddVirtualNic,AddVirtualSwit ch,AddVirtualSwitchPortGroup, FlipNetworkService, Remove-VirtualNic

You can quickly get started with the VI Java API. http.//vijava. sourceforge.net/doc/getstarted/tutorial.htm

---

There are many samples that can be found, such as the following: http://vijava.svn.sourceforge.net/viewvc/vijava/trunk/ src/com/vmware/vim25/mo/samples/

5.6.2 Skeletal Outline of the Master Deployment Script

This script is based on using Apache Ant and VI-Java-API

```
<project name="MyProject" default="runMasterDeploymentScript" basedir=".">

<target name ="runMasterDeploymentScript" depends="takeSnapshotOfV
M,switchLoadBalancer, deployDBChanges, deployWARFile ">
</target>
<target name="takeSnapshotOfVM">
        <java
         fork="true"
         maxmemory="256m"
         jvm="${JavaHome}"
         classname="yourcompay.SnapshotManager" >
         <arg value="-takeSnapshot"/> <arg value="${vcenterURL}"/>
```

```xml
        <arg value="${adminUsername}"/> <arg value="${adminPwd}"/>
        <arg value="${vmname}"/> <arg value="${snapshotname}"/>
        <arg value="${desc}"/>
                    <classpath>
                    <pathelement path="${VIJavaHome}/vijava2120100715.jar"/>
                    </classpath>
            </java>
 </target>
 <target name="switchLoadBalancer">
  <!-- invoke Load balancer API or shell script to switch from Production-1 to
Production-2, refer to 1.33.4-->
 </target>
<target name="deployDbChanges">
 <sql driver="org.database.jdbcDriver" url="jdbc:database-url" userid="sa"
  password="pass" >
  <transaction src="data1.sql"/>
</sql>
</target>
 <target name="deployWARFile">
 <!--use Ant Copy task to copy file to destination and Ant Unzip task to extract
</target>

<target name="rollBackToPriorSnapshot">
        <java
         fork="true"
         maxmemory="256m"
        jvm="${JavaHome}"
        classname="yourcompay.SnapshotManager" >
                <arg value="-revertSnapshot"/>
                <arg value="${vcenterURL}/>
   <arg value="${adminUsername}"/> <arg value="${adminPwd}/>
   <arg value="${vmname}"/> <arg value="${snapshotname
                <classpath>
                <pathelement path="${VIJavaHome}/vijava2120100715.jar"/>
                </classpath>
        </java>
</target>
</project>
```

5.6.3 How to Interact with a VM Using the VI-Java-API

5.6.3.1. Take a Snapshot of a VM

You can either wrap these calls in a Java command-line call or include them in an Ant Java task. Use the Service Instance object to connect to vCenter. This is then used to execute various VM functionalities.

```java
Import com.vmware.vim25.*;
//note you will need vijava2120100715.jar for example on your CLASSPATH
Public class SnapshotManager {
//.....
public ServiceInstance getServiceInstance(
String vcenterURL, String adminUsername, String adminPwd)
{
 ServiceInstance si = null;
 try {
 si = new ServiceInstance(new URL(vcenterURL), adminUsername, adminPwd,
true);
 } catch (RemoteException e) {
   e.printStackTrace();
 } catch (MalformedURLException e) {
   e.printStackTrace();
 }
 return si;
}
Public static void main(String[] args)
{
 SnapshotManager ssm = new SnapshotManager();
 If (arg[0].equals("takeSnapshot")
 {
 //Ssm.takeSnapshotOfVM( vcenterURL, adminUsername,adminPwd,
 vmname,snapshotname, desc)
 ssm.takeSnapshotOfVM( arg[1], arg[2],arg[3], arg[4],arg[5], arg[6])
 }else if (arg[0].equals("revertSnapshot"))
 {
   ssm. revertToSnapshotOfVM( arg[1], arg[2],arg[3], arg[4],arg[5])
 }
}
```

Using the getServiceInstance method you can take snapshot of a VM:

```java
public String takeSnapShotOfVM( String vcenterURL, String adminUsername,
String adminPwd, String vmname, String snapshotname, String desc)
{
 ServiceInstance si = getServiceInstance(vcenterURL, adminUsername, admin-
Pwd);
 Folder rootFolder = si.getRootFolder();
 String returnFlag = null;
 try {
 VirtualMachine vm = (VirtualMachine) new InventoryNavigator(
      rootFolder).searchManagedEntity(VIRTUAL_MACHINE, vmname);
 Task task = vm.createSnapshot_Task(snapshotname, desc, false, false);
 if(task.waitForTask()==Task.SUCCESS)
 {
  returnFlag = Task.SUCCESS;
 }else
 {
  returnFlag = "failure";
 }
  } catch (InterruptedException e) {
    // other catch clauses omitted for brevity...
    // other catch clauses go here...
  }
  return returnFlag; }
```

If you need to take snapshots for multiple VMs, you can iterate the method N times to get a snapshot for the set of VMs.

5.6.3.2. Revert to a Snapshot

```
public String revertToSnapshotOfVM(
String vcenterURL, String adminUsername,
String adminPwd, String vmname, String snapshotname)
{
        String returnFlag = null;
        try {
        ServiceInstance si = getServiceInstance(vcenterURL, adminUsername,
adminPwd);
        Folder rootFolder = si.getRootFolder();

        VirtualMachine vm =
(VirtualMachine) new InventoryNavigator(rootFolder).searchManagedEntity(
"VirtualMachine", vmname);

        VirtualMachineSnapshot vmsnap = getSnapshotInTree(vm, snapshotname);
        if(vmsnap!=null)
        {
                Task task;
                task = vmsnap.revertToSnapshot_Task(null);
            if(task.waitForTask()==Task.SUCCESS)
            {
                    System.out.println("Reverted to snapshot:"+ snapshotname);
                    returnFlag = Task.SUCCESS;
                    }
        }

        } catch (InvalidProperty e1) {
                // other catch clauses omitted for brevity…

                }
                return returnFlag;
        }
```

The above revertToSnapshotOfVM method depends on getSnap-shotInTree, the full source listing is provided by SourceForge at the following:

http://vijava.svn.sourceforge.net/viewvc/vijava/trunk/src/com/vmware/vim25/mo/samples/vm/VMSnapshot.java?revision=189&view=markup

5.6.4 Interact with Load Balancer

Depending on which load balancers you use, you will need to refer to the appropriate documentation provided by the vendor for using the API and management interface.

The following load balancers have a virtual appliance model for VMware vSphere:

- F5 VMware vSphere Solutions, refer to: http://www.f5.com/solutions/applications/vmware/vsphere/
- Zeus product information, refer to: http://www.zeus.com/products/load-balancer
- Coyote Point Equalizer VLB and Equalizer VLB Advanced product information, refer to: http://www.coyotepoint.com/

5.7 Conclusion

There are various ways to achieve a highly available enterprise Java application using VMware technology. The following features are critical to achieving optimal availability:

- Fully automated application deployment via master deployment script as discussed in this chapter. This is critical to reducing the scheduled downtime during releases.
- Ability to hot plug/hot add CPU and memory of a VM at runtime without an outage.
- Ability to add new hosts and VMs and have them automatically discovered and configured by the load balancer.
- Ability to implement a disaster-recovery solution using VMware vCenter Site Recovery Manager and load-balancer technology.

You can complement these features with your Java application server's cluster configuration. Figure 29 shows an architecture that is capable of 99.99 percent uptime. This assumes that other parts of the Infrastructure have adequate redundancy, there are no performance issues within Java-application code, and the database server also has an uptime of 99.99 percent.

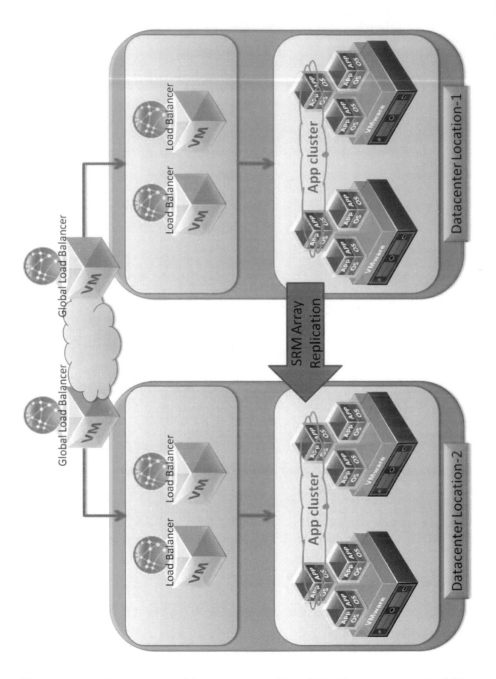

Figure 29: *Shows an architecture capable of 99.99 percent availability*

Chapter 6

Enterprise Java on VMware Best Practices

6.1 Overview

This chapter provides information about best practices for deploying enterprise Java applications on VMware, including key best-practice considerations for architecture, performance, design and sizing, and high availability. This information is intended to help IT architects successfully deploy and run Java environments on VMware vSphere™.

6.2 Purpose

The recommendations in this chapter are not specific to any particular set of hardware or to the size and scope of any particular implementation. The best practices in this chapter provide guidance only, and do not represent strict design requirements because enterprise Java application requirements can vary from one implementation to another. However, the guidelines do form a good foundation on which you can build—many VMware customers have used these guidelines to successfully virtualize their enterprise Java applications. This chapter focuses on details about the deployment of enterprise Java applications on VMware vSphere, and it is not necessarily a best-practice guide for pure Java. For specific Java best practices, refer to the vendor documentation for the JVM you are using.

Virtualizing enterprise Java applications does not require a change in your Java coding paradigm, and any performance enhancements that you have done on physical are transferrable, as is the vSphere deployed instance of your application.

6.3 Scope

This chapter covers the following topics:

- Enterprise Java Applications on vSphere Architecture: This section provides high-level best-practice architecture for running enterprise Java applications on vSphere.
- Enterprise Java Applications on vSphere Best Practices: This section provides best-practice guidelines for properly preparing the vSphere platform to run enterprise Java applications on vSphere. Best practices for the design and sizing of VMs, guest-OS tips, CPU, memory, storage, networking, and useful JVM tuning parameters are presented. Also covered are the various high-availability features in vSphere, including VMware ESX™ host clusters, resource pools (*horizontal scalability* and *vertical scalability*) along with the VMware Distributed Resource Scheduler (DRS).

6.4 Enterprise Java Applications on vSphere Architecture

This section provides details on best-practice architecture for enterprise Java applications running on vSphere. Enterprise Java applications are made of four main tiers. These are the following:

- Load Balancers tier
- Web Servers tier
- Java Application Server tier
- DB Server tier

A highly scalable and robust Java application has all of these tiers running in VMware vSphere in order to reap the full benefits of scalability features offered by vSphere. Figure 30 shows a multitier, fully virtualized enterprise Java applications architecture running on VMware vSphere.

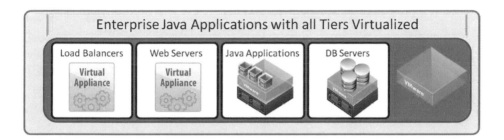

Figure 30: *Shows a multitier virtualized enterprise Java application architecture*

Each one of these tiers is running in a VM that is managed by VMware vSphere, which forms the key building foundation. Best practices are discussed in this chapter for vSphere features such as VMware HA, DRS, VMware vMotion™, resource pools, hot plug/hot add, networking, and storage.

The following are key architectural attributes of each tier:

- Load Balancer tier: Increasingly feature-rich load balancers are available that provide various load-balancing algorithms and API integration with VMware vSphere. This allows the enterprise Java application architecture to scale on demand as traffic bursts occur.
- Web Server tier: This tier must be appropriately tuned, with the right number of HTTP threads to service your anticipated traffic demands.
- Java Application Server tier: Many of the commonly used application servers have mechanisms to help you tune the Java virtual machine to meet traffic demands. If you have

already tuned the available Java threads, JDBC configurations, and various JVM and GC parameters on physical machines, the tuning information is transferrable as is to the virtualized version of the enterprise Java applications.

- DB Server tier: Critical to meeting the uptime SLA of enterprise Java applications is having appropriate high-availability architecture for the DB server. DB servers can benefit from running on vSphere—see the best practices for your DB server on vSphere. This chapter covers best practices on JDBC connection-pool-tuning requirements at the Java application server level that the DB server needs to accommodate.

6.5 Enterprise Java Applications on vSphere Best Practices

6.5.1 VM Sizing and Configuration Best Practices Overview

Enterprise Java applications are highly customizable, and consequently, a performance test has to be conducted to establish best sizing.

It is a best practice to establish the size of your VM, in terms of vCPU, memory and how many JVMs are needed, by conducting a thorough performance test that mimics your production-workload profile. The resulting VM from the vertical scalability (scale-up) performance test is referred to as the building-block VM. The building-block VM is a good candidate template on which scaled-out (horizontally scaled) VMs can be based.

6.5.2 vCPU for VMs Best Practices

Best Practice	Description
BP1: VM Sizing and VM-to-JVM ratio through a performance load test	Establish a workload profile and conduct a load test to measure how many JVMs you can stack on a particular sized VM. In this test, establish a best-case scenario of how many concurrent transactions you can push through a configuration before it can be safely deemed a good candidate for scaling horizontally in an application cluster.
BP2: VM vCPU CPU overcommit	For performance-critical enterprise Java applications VMs in production, make sure the total number of vCPUs assigned to all of the virtual machines does not cause greater than 80 percent CPU utilization on the ESX host.
BP3: VM vCPU Do not oversubscribe to CPU cycles that you don't really need	If your performance load test determines, for example, 2-vCPU is adequate up to 70 percent CPU utilization, but instead you allocate 4-vCPU to your VM, then potentially you have 2-vCPUs idle, which is not optimal. If the exact workload is not known, size the virtual machine with a smaller number of vCPUs initially and increase the number later, if necessary.

6.5.3 VM Memory-Size Best Practice

To understand how to size memory for a VM, you must understand the memory requirements of Java and various segments within it. Figure 31 provides an illustration of these separate memory areas.

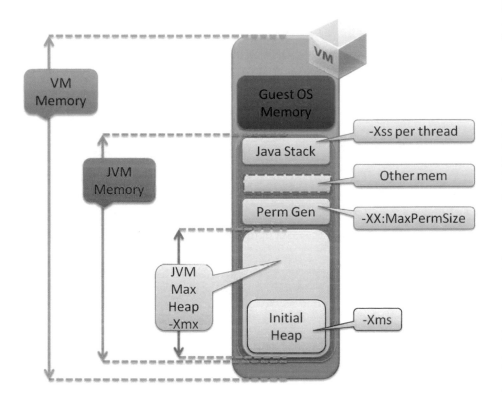

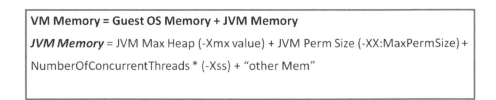

VM Memory = Guest OS Memory + JVM Memory

JVM Memory = JVM Max Heap (-Xmx value) + JVM Perm Size (-XX:MaxPermSize) + NumberOfConcurrentThreads * (-Xss) + "other Mem"

Figure 31: *Shows a single-sun HotSpot JVM deployed on one VM*

The JVM memory, or sometimes commonly referenced as the Java process memory, is made of direct memory (PermGen, Java Stack, and Other Memory), and non-direct memory areas (Java heap). Direct memory is allocated natively from the Guest OS memory, while the non-direct is virtual address space memory known as the Java heap. The Java heap is a very active area where objects are being copied around -Java objects live initially in the young generation and then copied to survivor spaces where eventually are copied to the tenured space. Objects that survive a garbage collection (or GC process that is actively collecting garbage or de-referenced objects) are copied to tenured space. This form of active memory space needs to have reserved memory allocated to it as it the JVM through the GC process is actively managing the movement of objects.

The Java heap (non direct memory) is configured using –Xmx, this governs the maximum amount of heap, while the initial heap is configured with –Xms.

This equation in Figure 31 assumes the following:

- *Perm Gen* is an area that is in addition to the -Xmx (*max heap*) value and is not GCed, as it holds the class-level information about the code. IBM JVMs do not have a Perm Gen area.
- The above VM Memory formula is an approximation of the main areas allocated.
- *"Other-mem"* refers to the following: To more accurately size you need to load test the Java application for additional memory requirements that may be allocated due to NIO buffers: JIT code cache, classloaders, and verifiers. In particular, some Java applications may use NIO buffers, which can have huge additional memory demands.
- The contents of a direct buffer are allocated from the guest operating system memory instead of the Java heap, and non-direct buffers are copied into direct buffers for native I/O operations. Use load testing to appropriately size the effect of these buffers.

- If you have multiple JVMs (N JVMs) on a VM then: *VM memory = guest OS memory + N * JVM memory.*

Figure 32 illustrates the memory segments for an IBM JVM, The main difference is the PermGen area, where all the class-level information is kept and managed inside the heap as linked lists that get eventually de-referenced/GCed if or when the class is unloaded. This implies that if you compare the –Xmx heap utilization between Sun HotSpot JVM versus IBM JVM, you will find the heap for the IBM JVM slightly higher due to this. At any rate this area is not a significant portion of the memory. But it is allocated from the heap instead of native memory. It is important to note that this area is not really called Perm-Gen in IBM JVM terminology, but we use it for ease of illustration, and so that anyone familiar with HotSpot concepts can easily interpret this.

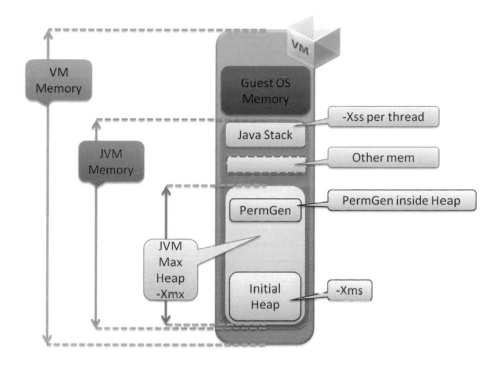

VM Memory = Guest OS Memory + JVM Memory

JVM Memory =

JVM Max Heap (-Xmx value) + NumberOfConcurrentThreads * (-Xss) + "otherMem"

Figure 32: *Shows single IBM JVM on one VM*

NOTE: PermGen is omitted from the equation, as it is part of the value of –Xmx for IBM JVMs since it is inside the heap. The PermGen area, as explained earlier, is not a separate area within the heap. It is simply a linked list that gets managed like any other object in the heap.

Best Practice	Description
BP4: VM memory sizing	Whether you are using Windows or Linux as your guest OS, refer to the technical specification of the various vendors for memory requirements. It is common to see the guest OS allocated about 1GB in addition to the JVM memory size. However, each installation may have additional processes running on it (for example, monitoring agents), and you need to accommodate their memory requirements as well. Figure 31 shows the various segments of JVM and VM memory, and the formula summarizes VM Memory as the following: VM Memory (needed) = guest OS memory + JVM Memory, where JVM Memory = JVM Max Heap (-Xmx value) + Perm Gen (-XX:MaxPermSize) + NumberOfConcurrentThreads * (-Xss) + "other mem" The -Xmx value is the value that you found during load testing for your application on physical servers. This value does not need to change when moving to a virtualized environment. Load testing your application when deployed on vSphere will help confirm the best -Xmx value. It is recommended that you do not overcommit memory because the JVM memory is an active space where objects are constantly being created and garbage collected. Such an active

memory space requires its memory to be available all the time. If you overcommit, memory ballooning or swapping may occur and impede performance.
ESX host employs two distinct techniques for dynamically expanding or contracting the amount of memory allocated to virtual machines.

The first method is known as memory *balloon driver* (vmmemctl). This is loaded from the VMware Tools package into the guest operating system running in a virtual machine. The second method involves paging from a virtual machine to a server swap file, without any involvement by the guest operating system.

In the page-swapping method, when you power on a virtual machine, a corresponding swap file is created and placed in the same location as the virtual machine configuration file (VMX file). The virtual machine can power on only when the swap file is available. ESX hosts use swapping to forcibly reclaim memory from a virtual machine when no balloon driver is available. The balloon driver may be unavailable either because VMware Tools is not installed, or because the driver is disabled or not running. For optimum performance, ESX uses the balloon approach whenever possible. However, swapping is used when the driver is temporarily unable to reclaim memory quickly enough to satisfy current system demands. Because the memory is being swapped out to disk, there

Best Practice	Description
	is a significant performance penalty when the swapping technique is used. Therefore, it is recommended that the balloon driver is always enabled, but monitor this to verify that it is not getting invoked as that memory is overcommitted. Both ballooning and swapping should be prevented for Java applications. To prevent ballooning and swapping, refer to BP5: Set memory reservation for VM needs.
BP5:Set memory reservation for VM memory needs	JVMs running on VMs have an active heap space requirement that must always be present in physical memory. Use the VMware vSphere Client to set the reservation equal to the needed VM memory.
	Reservation Memory = VM Memory = guest OS Memory + JVM Memory
	You may set this reservation to the active memory being used by the VM for a more efficient use of the amount of memory available. Or a simpler approach is to set the reservation equal to the total configured memory of the VM.

BP6: Use large memory pages	Large memory pages help performance by optimizing the use of the Translation Look-aside Buffer (TLB), where virtual-to-physical address translations are performed. Use large memory pages as supported by your JVM and your guest operating system. The operating system and the JVM must be informed that you want to use large memory pages, as is the case when using large pages in physical systems. Set the -XX:+UseLargePages at the JVM level for Sun HotSpot. On the IBM JVM it is -Xlp, and JRockit -XXlargePages. You also need to enable this at the guest OS level. For information, see the following: ***http://www.vmware.com/files/pdf/large_pg_performance***

6.6 VM Memory and JVM Memory-Sizing Example

In this section an actual sizing example based on the information presented earlier is shown. Let's take the generalized equation presented in Figure 34, and build an actual sizing example:

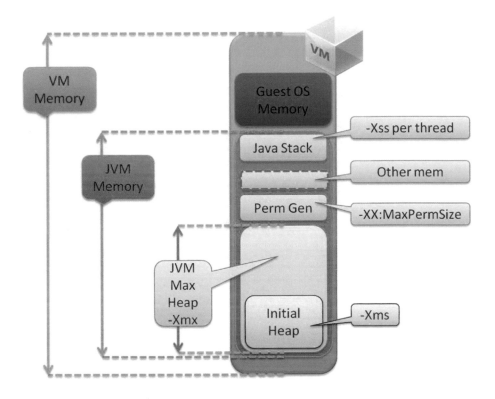

Figure 33: *Shows a virtual machine (VM) with one HotSpot JVM.*

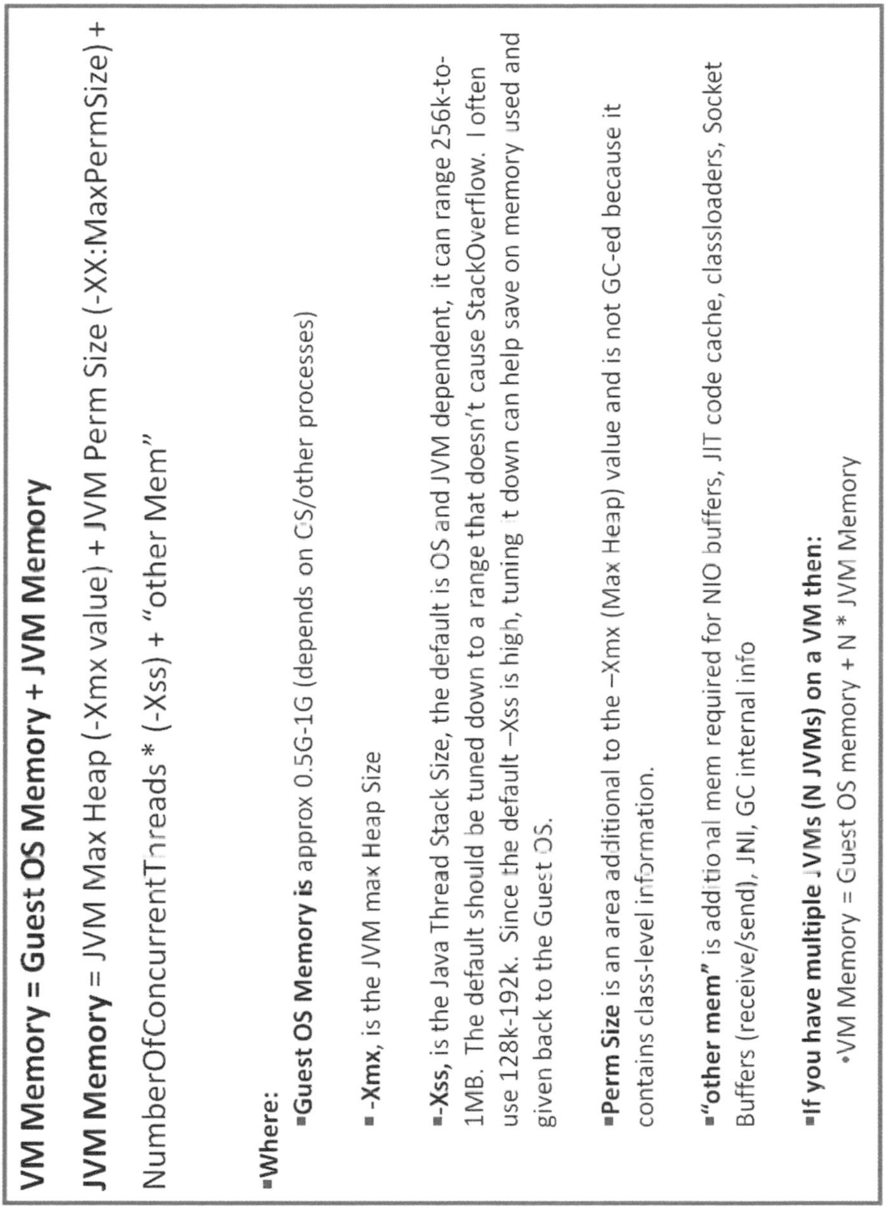

VM Memory = Guest OS Memory + JVM Memory

JVM Memory = JVM Max Heap (-Xmx value) + JVM Perm Size (-XX:MaxPermSize) + NumberOfConcurrentThreads * (-Xss) + "other Mem"

- Where:
  - **Guest OS Memory is** approx 0.5G-1G (depends on CS/other processes)

  - **-Xmx,** is the JVM max Heap Size

  - **-Xss,** is the Java Thread Stack Size, the default is OS and JVM dependent, it can range 256k-to-1MB. The default should be tuned down to a range that doesn't cause StackOverflow. I often use 128k-192k. Since the default -Xss is high, tuning t down can help save on memory used and given back to the Guest OS.

  - **Perm Size** is an area additional to the -Xmx (Max Heap) value and is not GC-ed because it contains class-level information.

  - **"other mem"** is additional mem required for NIO buffers, JIT code cache, classloaders, Socket Buffers (receive/send), JNI, GC internal info

  - **If you have multiple JVMs (N JVMs) on a VM then:**
    - •VM Memory = Guest OS memory + N * JVM Memory

Figure 34: *Shows the generalized memory-sizing equation of all the memory segments shown in* **Figure 33**

Let's assume that, through load testing, a JVM max heap (-Xmx) of 4096m has been determined as necessary.

So you would proceed to size according to the following:

- Set -Xmx4096m, also set –Xms4096m
- Set –XX:MaxPermSize=256m, you have chosen to use –XX:MaxPermSize of 256m, which is a common number and depends on the memory footprint of the class-level information within your Java application code base.
- The other segment of NumberOfConcurrentThreads*(-Xss) depends largely on NumberOfConcurrentThreads the JVM will process, and the –Xss value you have chosen. A common range of –Xss is 128k-192k.
  - Note: -Xss is application dependent; if the stack is not sized correctly you will get a StackOverflow. As noted earlier, the default value is sometimes quite large, and you can benefit from sizing it down to help save on memory consumption.
  - If, for example, you choose a 4vCPU VM, and assume NumberOfConcurrentThreads is four, then 4*192k => 768k (assuming you set –Xss to 192k)
    - This implies the number of simultaneous threads can be executed against a vCPU and a hence Java thread will occupy a vCPU cycle when executing.
    - Note: Regardless of how many Java Threads you have configured at the application server layer, only 4 concurrent threads can execute on the 4vCPU VM at any given instance of time. Now that doesn't mean you can only setup a Java Thread pool of 4 in your application - the relationship between how many Java threads to vCPU will depend on how vCPU resource consuming is your application and how much of the vCPU cycle the Java Threads

will consume. However, in terms of memory consumption it is true to say that at any instance in time the memory consumption of the thread stack is accurately calculated as 4* (-Xss) for stack memory as it is dictated by the number of vCPUs. **In practice though for example, you may have a enterprise Java application deployed on an application server where you have configured 100 threads, a more accurate calculation of native memory consumed by the Java threads over the course of the application run cycle/load test is** *100 Java Threads * (-Xss)*, **and hence in our example it would be more accurate to calculate the native memory consumption by Java threads as: 100*192k=>19.2M** To understand impact – Xss area, and number of Java threads on native memory that is outside the heap, a good load testing will give you a practical measure. The above equation and example should be your starting point.

- Assume the OS has a requirement of about 500m to run as per the OS spec
- Total JVM memory (Java process memory) = 4096m (-Xmx) + 256m (–XX:MaxPermSize) + 4*192k (NumberOf ConcurrentThreads*-Xss) + "other mem"
    - o Therefore, JVM memory is approximately 4096m+256m+0.768m + "other mem" = 4352.768m + "other mem"
    - o Now typically "other mem" is not significant. However, it can be quite large if the application uses lots of NIO buffers and socket buffers. Otherwise assuming about 5 percent of the total JVM process memory (i.e., 5 percent * 4352.768= 217m), should be enough,

> although proper load testing should be used to verify.
> - o This now implies that JVM process memory is 4352.768m+217m=4570m
- Now to determine the VM memory, assume you are using Linux with no other significant process running, and only this single Java process, your total configured memory for the VM translates to the following: VM memory = 4570m + 500m = 5070m
- Next you should set the VM memory as the memory reservation. You can choose to set the memory reservation as 5070m. However, over time you should monitory the active memory used by the VM that houses this JVM process and adjust the memory reservation to that active memory value, which could be less than 5070m.

NOTE: A common misconception is to assume that this −Xmx value is equal to the Java process memory needed, but clearly as described by the equation in Figure 31 and in Figure 34, the JVM memory (or Java process memory) is greater than the JVM max heap (greater than −Xmx), and this is due to the other additional segments that make up the memory space of the total Java process such as JVM Perm Size, NumberOfConcurrentThreads*(-Xss), and the "other memory" section.

Refer to Figure 35 for an illustration of the above sizing example.

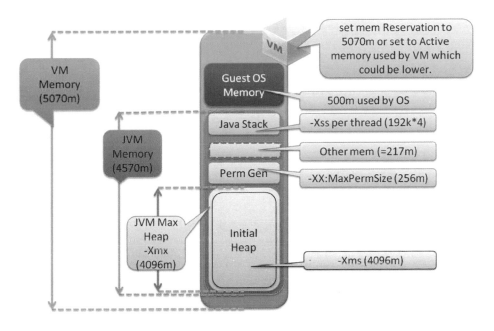

Figure 35: *Shows an actual sizing example we just discussed above, in order to illustrate the amount of memory each segment has been set to.*

6.6.1 BP5: How to Set Memory Reservation

Set the memory-reservation value in the vSphere client to the size of memory for the virtual machine. Refer to Figure 35 for an illustration of the above sizing example.

Figure 35, the memory reservation is set to 5070MB. This virtual machine is always allocated this amount of memory on any ESX host on which it runs.

To set the memory reservation, select the VM, right-click and select **Edit Settings** > **Resources** tab. Figure 36 shows how to set the memory reservation for a virtual machine in the vSphere Client.

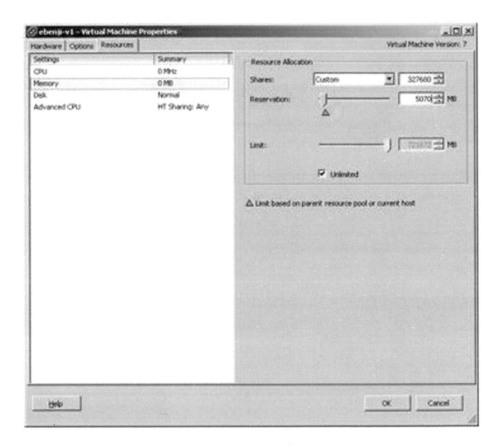

Figure 36: *Shows how to set the memory reservation*

6.6.2 VM Timekeeping Best Practices

Best Practice	Description
BP7: Timekeeping Use NTP Source	Timekeeping can be different in virtual machines than on physical machines for a variety of reasons (see Timekeeping in VMware Virtual Machines: VMware ESX 4.0/ESXi 4.0, VMware Workstation 7.0 (http://www.vmware.com/files/pdf/Timekeeping). Timekeeping can have an effect on Java programs if they are sensitive to accurate measurements over periods of time, or if they need a timestamp that is within an exact tolerance (such as a timestamp on a shared document or data item). VMware Tools contains features that are installable into the guest operating system to enable time synchronization, and the use of those tools is recommended. The effects of timer interrupts are also discussed, as the frequency of those interruptions can have an effect on the performance of your Java application.

6.6.3 Configuration for Timekeeping Best Practices

- Synchronize the time on the ESX host with an NTP source. See the following: http://www.vmware.com/files/pdf/Timekeeping.
- Synchronize the time in the virtual machine's guest operating system:
- For Linux guest operating systems using an external NTP source, see the following: http://www.vmware.com/files/pdf/Timekeeping.
- For Windows guest operating systems use W32Time. Refer to your Windows administration guide for detailed information.

- Lower the clock interrupt rate on the virtual CPUs in your virtual machines by using a guest operating system that allows lower timer interrupts. Examples of such operating systems are RHEL 4.7 and later, RHEL 5.2 and later, and the SuSE Linux Enterprise Server 10 SP2. See the following: http://kb.vmware.com/selfservice/microsites/search.do?cmd=displayKC&docType=kc&externalId=1006427&sliceId=1&docTypeID=DT_KB_1_1&dialogID=131835784&stateId=0%200%20131839654 for more information on timekeeping best practices for Linux.

- Use the Java features for lower resolution timing that are supplied by your JVM, such as the option for the Sun JVM on Windows guest operating systems:
  o `-XX:+ForceTimeHighResolution`

- You can also set the _JAVA_OPTIONS variable to this value on Windows operating systems using the technique given (which is useful in cases where you cannot easily change the Java command line).

- The following is an example of how to set the Sun JVM option. To set the _JAVA_OPTIONS environment variable:
  o Click **Start** > **Settings** > **Control Panel** > **System** > **Advanced** > **Environment Variables**.
  o Click **New** under **System Variables**. The variable name is `_JAVA_OPTIONS.` The variable value is `-XX:+ForceTimeHighResolution.`
  o Reboot the guest operating system to properly propagate the variable.
  o Avoid using the `/usepmtimer` option in the `boot.ini` system configuration for Windows guest operating systems that use an SMP HAL.

6.6.5 Vertical Scalability Best Practices

If an enterprise Java application deployed on vSphere experiences heavy CPU utilization, and you have determined that an increase in the vCPU count will help resolve the saturation, you can use vSphere hot add to add additional vCPU.

Best Practice	Description
BP8: Hot Add CPU/ Memory	VMs with a guest OS that supports hot add CPU and hot add memory can take advantage of the ability to change the VM configuration at runtime without any interruption to VM operations. This is particularly useful when you are trying to increase the ability of the VM to handle more traffic.
	Plan ahead and enable this feature. The VM must be turned off to have the hot-plug feature enabled, but when enabled you can hot add CPU and hot add memory at runtime without VM shutdown (if the guest OS supports it).
	When you need to increase Java heap space, you usually to increase vCPU count to get the best GC cycle performance. Keep in mind that there are many other aspects to GC tuning, and you should refer to your JVM documentation.

6.6.5 Horizontal Scalability, Clusters, and Pools Best Practices

Enterprise Java applications deployed on VMware vSphere can benefit from using vSphere features for horizontal scalability using ESX host clusters, resource pools, host affinity, and DRS.

Best Practice	Description
BP9: Use ESX host cluster	To enable better scalability, use ESX host clusters. When creating clusters enable VMware HA and VMware DRS: VMware HA—Detects failures and provides rapid recovery for the VM running in a cluster. Core functionality includes host monitoring and VM monitoring to minimize downtime. VMware DRS—Enables vCenter Server to manage hosts as an aggregate pool of resources. Cluster resources can be divided into smaller pools for users, groups, and VMs. It enables vCenter to manage the assignment of VMs to hosts automatically, suggesting placement when VMs are powered on, and migrating running VMs to balance load and enforce allocation policies. Enable EVC (for either Intel or AMD). EVC is Enhanced vMotion Compatibility; it configures a cluster and its hosts to maximize vMotion compatibility. When EVC is enabled, only hosts that are compatible with those in the cluster may be added to the cluster.

Best Practice	Description
BP10: Use resource pools	Multiple resource pools can be used within a cluster to manage compute-resource consumption by either reserving the needed memory for the VMs within a resource pool or by limiting or restricting it to a certain level. This feature also helps you meet quality of service and requirements. For example, you can create a Tier-2 resource pool for the less critical applications and a Tier-1 resource pool for business-critical applications.
BP11: Affinity rules	In addition to exiting anti-affinity rules, the VM-Host affinity rule was introduced in vSphere 4.1. The VM-Host affinity rule provides the ability to place VMs on a subset of hosts in a cluster. This is very useful in honoring ISV licensing requirements. Rules can be created so that VMs run on ESX hosts in different blades for higher availability. Conversely, limit the ESX host to one blade in case network traffic between the VMs needs to be optimized by keeping them in one chassis location.
BP12: Use vSphere-aware load balancers	vSphere makes it easy to add resources such as host and VMs at runtime. It is possible to provision these ahead of time. However, it is simpler if you use a load balancer that is able to integrate with vSphere APIs to detect the newly added VMs and add them to its application load-balancing pools without downtime.

6.6.6 Inter-tier Configuration Best Practices

As discussed in section 6.4 of this chapter, there are four critical technology tiers that sit on top of vSphere. These tiers are the Load Balancer tier, the Web Server tier, the Java Application Server tier, and the DB Server tier. The configurations for compute resources at each tier must translate to an equitable configuration at the next tier. For example, if the Web Server tier is configured to handle 100 HTTP requests per second, then of those requests you must determine how many Java application server threads are needed, and in turn how many DB connections are needed in the JDBC Pool configuration.

Best Practice	Description
BP13: Establish appropriate thread ratios that prevents bottlenecks (HTTP threads:Java threads:DB connections)	This is the ratio of HTTP threads to Java threads to DB connections. Establish initial setup by assuming that each layer requires a 1:1:1 ratio of HTTP threads:Java Threads:DB-connections. Based on the response time and throughput numbers, adjust each of these properties accordingly until you have satisfied your SLA objectives. For example, if you have one hundred HTTP requests submitted to the Web server initially, assume that all of these will have an interaction with Java threads, and in turn, DB connections. Of course, in reality, during your benchmark you will find that not all HTTP threads are submitted to the Java application server. In turn, not all Java application server threads each require a DB connection. That is, you may find your ratio for one hundred requests translates to one hundred HTTP threads:twenty-five Java threads:ten Db connections. This depends on the nature of your enterprise Java application behaviour. Benchmarking helps you establish this ratio.

Best Practice	Description
BP14: Load-balancer algorithm choice and VM symmetry	Take into account the available algorithms of your load balancer. Make sure that when using the scale-out approach, all of your VMs are receiving an equal share of the traffic. Some industry standard algorithms are Round Robin, Weighted Round Robin, Least Connections, and Least Response Time. You may want to initially default to Least Connections and then adjust as you see fit in your load-test iterations. Keep your VMs symmetrical in terms of the size of compute resource. For example, if you decide to use 2-vCPU VMs as a repeatable, horizontally scalable building block, this helps with your load-balancing algorithm, working more effectively, as opposed to as if there were a pool of non-symmetrical VMs for one particular application. That is, mixing 2-vCPU VMs with 4-vCPU VMs in one load-balancer-facing pool is non-symmetrical, and the load balancer has no notion of weighing this unless you configure for it at the load-balancer level, which is time consuming.

6.6.7 High-level vSphere Best Practices

It is important to follow the best practices. See the following: http://www.vmware.com/pdf/Perf_Best_Practices_vSphere4.0.pdf

The following is a summary of some of the key networking, storage, and hardware-related best practices that are commonly used.

6.6.7.1 vSphere Networking Best Practices

Best Practice	Description
BP15: vSphere networking	Follow vSphere networking best practices. In addition, see the following: http://www.vmware.com/pdf/Perf_Best_Practices_vSphere4.0.pdf Refer to VMware virtual networking concepts and best practices: http://www.vmworld.com/docs/DOC-5122.

6.6.7.1 vSphere Storage Best Practices

Best Practice	Description
BP16: vSphere storage	VMware recommends a minimum of four paths from an ESX host to a storage array, which means the host requires at least two HBA ports. Follow vSphere storage best practices. For a detailed description of VMware storage best practices refer to the VMware SAN System Deployment and Design Guide: http://www.vmware.com/files/pdf/techpaper/SAN

6.6.8 vSphere Server Hardware Configuration Best Practices

Best Practice	Description
BP17: ESX Host hardware	For hardware configuration best practices, refer to VMware vCenter Server Performance and Best Practices Guide: http://www.vmware.com/files/pdf/tech-paper/vsp_41_perf_VC_Best_Practices.pdf. Also see The CPU Scheduler in VMware ESX4.1 Guide: http://www.vmware.com/files/pdf/techpaper/VMW_vSphere41_cpu_schedule_ESX Disable any other power-saving mode in the BIOS. NUMA Considerations – IBM (X-Architecture), AMD (Opteron-based), and Intel (Nehalem) non-uniform memory access (NUMA) systems are supported by ESX. On AMD Opteron-based systems, such as the HP ProLiant DL585 Server, BIOS settings for node interleaving determine whether the system behaves like a NUMA system or like a uniform memory-accessing (UMA) system. By default, ESX NUMA scheduling and related optimizations are enabled only on systems with a total of at least four CPU cores and with at least two CPU cores per NUMA node. Virtual machines with a number of vCPUs equal to or less than the number of cores in each NUMA node are managed by the NUMA scheduler and have the best performance. Hardware Bios – Verify the BIOS is set to enable all populated sockets, and enable all cores in each socket. Enable Turbo Mode if your processors support it. Make sure hyper-threading is enabled in the BIOS.

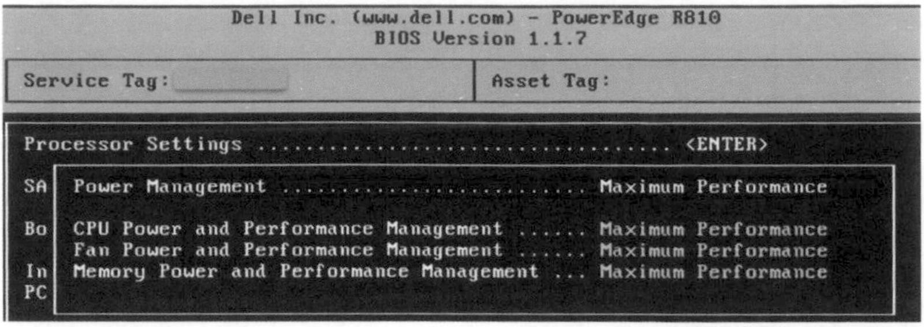

Figure 37: *Shows an example of disabling power-saving mode, and enabling maximum performance mode for PowerEdge R810 in the Bios.*

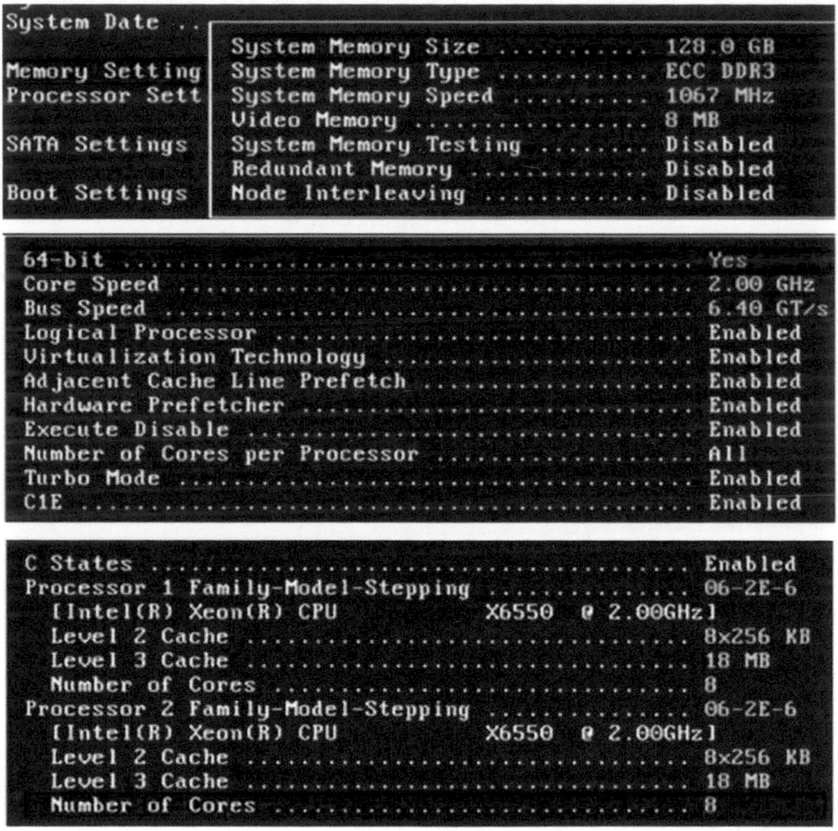

Figure 38: *Shows ideal server BIOS settings for maximum performance*

In Figure 38, a Dell server configuration is shown where there are two Chips, each with eight physical cores. Hence, there are two NUMA nodes, each with eight physical cores wide, or sixteen logical cores since HT is enabled. This makes for a total of thirty-two logical processors across the two chips. When sizing for best NUMA locality, ESX is optimized to take advantage of NUMA locality. For further NUMA locality you can set a vmx file-level property called vsmpConsolidate.

How to set vsmpConsolidate: If it is certain that a workload in a virtual machine will benefit from cache sharing and does not benefit from larger cache capacity, the preference can be specified by enabling vSMP consolidation, which causes sibling vCPUs from a multiprocessor virtual machine to be scheduled within an LLC. Such a preference might not always be honored, depending on the availability of vCPUs.

To enable vSMP consolidation for a virtual machine, take the following steps in vSphere Client:

    a.   Right-click the virtual machine and select Edit Settings.

    b.   Select the Options tab.

    c.   Under Advanced, click General, and on the right, click the Configuration Parameters button.

    d.   Click Add Row. Add sched.cpu.vsmpConsolidate set to true.

    e.   For further details refer to http://www.vmware.com/resources/techresources/10131.

NOTE: There is also a flag –XX:+UseNUMA at the JVM level. This flag pertains more to enterprise Java applications running on physical and that are not virtualized. When enterprise Java applications are virtualized, this flag takes no effect since the underlying hardware architecture is not exposed by VMware to the guest OS, and there is no need for it as there are many NUMA optimizations within VMware vSphere. In fact, the VMware hypervisor has extensive optimizations to manage cache and NUMA affinity for VMs. When the number of vCPUs in a VM fits in a single NUMA node, the hypervisor tries, within the constraints of available memory, to allocate memory for the VM from that node. Even when a VM spans multiple NUMA nodes, the hypervisor will allocate memory from the nodes on which the VM is running.

Further, in this example HT is enabled and hence the 16 physical cores will show up as 32 logical cores. It is advisable when attempting to over-commit CPU because your workloads are peaking at different times, the vCPU calculation should be based on vCPU <= 1.25 pCPUs, where pCPUs is the number of physical cores available. It is also equally important to keep in mind that the architecture shown in Figure 38 is made of two sockets (each socket counts as 1 NUMA node, hence you have 2 NUMA nodes) with 8 cores each, this means it is best to only size up to a maximum of 8vCPU VMs for more effective NUMA locality. Now naturally most Java workloads perform well and within good SLA using 2vCPU and 4vCPU VMs. However, there are the occasional workloads that may need the larger VMs. It is best practices to not size your VMs larger than the total server RAM divided by number of NUMA nodes. For the example shown in Figure 38 you see a total system memory of 128G across 2 sockets, hence 2 NUMA nodes. This implies that each NUMA node will get 64G (128G divided by 2 NUMA nodes) of RAM and it is best practice to size VMs less than 64G RAM in order to ensure good NUMA locality.

One caveat here, in vSphere 5 the NUMA architecture will be exposed to the Guest OS, referred to as vNUMA, and this really pertains to database loads that need huge VMs and not so much for Java VMs where the sweet spot of VM sizing is 2 to 4 vCPUs and VM memory within the NUMA boundary.

Chapter 7

UNIX-to-Linux Migration Considerations

7.1 Overview

This chapter focuses on key considerations for IT architects who are in the process of migrating Java applications from UNIX to Linux as part of their VMware server-consolidation project. Due to Java's cross-platform portability, Java applications are prime candidates to be migrated first, with relatively low complexity and effort.

Constraints mentioned in this chapter are applicable for Java applications that migrate from one OS to another, regardless of whether they run on physical or virtualized machines—they are not limits imposed by virtualization. The Java application code and runtime paradigm does not change when you migrate to a virtualized system. In fact, a Java application or application WAR file can be deployed as is from its physical machine form onto a virtual machine (VM) without change.

Because Java is a cross-platform, portable language, you can take custom enterprise Java applications and run them on any OS. The caveat is that the platform that the OS is running on must have a platform-specific JVM from the target vendor.

The following are key considerations when migrating custom enterprise Java applications from UNIX to Linux:

- Java language considerations
- Java compilation considerations
- Java runtime JVM considerations

An FAQ is provided to answer frequently asked questions related to migrating Java applications to VMware vSphere™.

7.2 Migration Prerequisites

Migrations of enterprise Java applications are often part of an overall migration plan. It is assumed that you have satisfied the following prerequisites as part of an overall migration plan:

- You have a high-level plan for the migration process that considers all tiers of your enterprise, including both infrastructure and the software-application layer.
- You have an application-topology list of dependencies to highlight the network dependencies and any special port mapping.
- You have studied the inter-tier dependencies, such as communication between load balancer and Web server.
- You may choose to migrate the Web server in Phase One, migrate the Java application server in Phase Two, and migrate the database in Phase Three.

Because inter-tier communication is mostly via TCP/IP, these dependencies are not tied to an operating system, assuming the operating system has a compliant implementation. For example, a Java application server communicates with the database server via JDBC, which is an implementation that sits on top of TCP/IP and is not OS-dependent. This is equally true for Web servers communicating back with the Java-application servers via HTTPs.

7.3 Key Unix-to-Linux Java-migration Considerations

7.3.1 Overview

Perform the following steps when migrating.

- Review any potential file-separator or path-naming conventions as outlined in Section 7.3.2.

- Consider the code compilation and deployment strategy as discussed in Section 7.3.3.
- Review Section 7.3.4 for the outlined key runtime-tuning configurations that potentially have to be migrated, as they may not be supported across various operating systems.

The following sections provide examples. There may be other third-party, or other Java classes and libraries that you depend on. If so, you have to test for compliance at compilation and performance of runtime.

7.3.2 Language Syntax and APIs Considerations

The popularity of Java is mainly due to its having a commonly known syntax and a set of libraries that can be written once and that target multiple platforms. Keep the following in mind.

In both UNIX and Linux, the same file-separator and path-separator characters are used, so if you chose to not make any changes to your code, this is acceptable, and the code is still cross-portable. However, it is a good housekeeping practice to use the file separator within your Java-application code. Instead of using characters such as the slash (/) in UNIX or Linux for path separators, use the following: java.io.File available approach.

```
//my file separator is
String fileSeparator = java.io.File.Separator
```

Equally applicable is the use of File.pathSeparator. Instead of using a character such as the colon (:) for path separators, use the java.io available approach.

```
//my path separator is
String pathSeparator = java.io.File.pathSeparator
```

If using java.File.io.renameTo, this method is OS-platform dependant, so your test script should always check the code as follows:

```
//always check your renameTo file code in unit test code
if (oldfile.renameTo(newfile)) {
    // test passed – rename succeeded
}else{
    // test failed – rename didn't succeed
}
```

7.3.3 Java Compilation Considerations

Java applications can run on any OS, due to the inherent capability of the language. However, as part of the migration you will probably want to recompile based on your new target Linux JVM in order to have a better overall compliance, and to conform to good-deployment best practices.

Perhaps as part of the larger migration strategy you had to reconstruct your UNIX shell scripts. Also, the Java compilation and deployment scripts may have been included as part of the script-reconstruction exercise. Instead of just reconstructing or reformatting your Java compilation scripts to the new Linux shell format (which is also a valid approach), it may be beneficial to use Apache Ant (http://ant.apache.org/) scripting to write a coherent Java-application compilation and deployment script that is cross-platform compatible.

The following is an example of an Ant build.xml script used to compile Java source code. Refer to the highlighted Compile Ant target.

```
project name="MyProject" default="dist" basedir=".">
  <description>
    simple example build file
  </description>
  <!-- set global properties for this build -->
```

```
<property name="src" location="src"/>
<property name="build" location="build"/>
<property name="dist" location="dist"/>

<target name="init">
 <!-- Create the time stamp -->
 <tstamp/>
 <!-- Create the build directory structure used by compile -->
 <mkdir dir="${build}"/>
</target>

<target name="compile" depends="init"
  description="compile the source " >
 <!-- Compile the java code from ${src} into ${build} -->
 <javac srcdir="${src}" destdir="${build}"/>
</target>

<target name="dist" depends="compile"
  description="generate the distribution" >
 <!-- Create the distribution directory -->
 <mkdir dir="${dist}/lib"/>

 <!-- Put everything in ${build} into the MyProject-${DSTAMP}.jar file -->
 <jar jarfile="${dist}/lib/MyProject-${DSTAMP}.jar" basedir="${build}"/>
</target>

<target name="clean"
  description="clean up" >
 <!-- Delete the ${build} and ${dist} directory trees -->
 <delete dir="${build}"/>
 <delete dir="${dist}"/>
</target>
</project>
```

See the Apache Ant Manual (http://ant.apache.org/manual/index.html) for information about installing, using, and running Ant scripts. Also see the javac—Java programming language compiler manual page: (http://download.oracle.com/javase/6/docs/technotes/tools/solaris/javac.html).

7.3.4 Java Runtime Considerations

Depending on which UNIX platform you are migrating from, you will find that certain JVM and or OS runtime options are not available for you to configure. Though Java is cross-platform portable, because the target platform JVM is changing from one platform to another, it is recommended that you perform a load-test exercise to establish the new benchmark for your Java application. When migrating from one OS to another, even though Java is portable, it is advisable that you load test and profile the characteristics of your application under the new technology stack.

The areas that pose the most challenge to migration are the JVM options that can be set and that are not cross-OS portable. The following sections summarize which options are valid for Solaris, and/or Linux.

7.3.5 JVM Options Specific to Solaris and/or Linux

The following options are valid on Solaris and/or Linux. They are some of the common options that may surface and lead to questions during migrations from Solaris to Linux. The JVM options that don't migrate across are best to be omitted, and rely on your load testing to see the impact refer to Table 4 for the set of JVM Options that can and cannot be migrated across to Linux from Solaris.

Table 4: *Solaris vs. Linux -XX JVM Property Migration Compatibility*

Attribute	Impact	Solaris	Linux
-XX:AltStackSize =16384	Alternate signal stack size (in Kbytes). (Removed from Java 5.0.)	Yes	No
-XX:+MaxFDLimit	Bump the number of file descriptors to max.	Yes	No
-XX:+UseAltSigs	Use alternate signals instead of SIGUSR1 and SIGUSR2 for VM internal signals. (Introduced in Java 1.3.1 update 9, 1.4.1. Relevant to Solaris only.)	Yes	No
-XX:+UseBound Threads	Bind user-level threads to kernel threads.	Yes	No
-XX:+UseLWP Synchronization	Use LWP-based instead of thread-based synchronization.	Yes	No
-XX:+UseVM InterruptibleIO	Thread interrupt before or with EINTR for I/O operations results in OS_INTRPT.	Yes	No

Attribute	Impact	Solaris	Linux
-XX:-ExtendedDTrace Probes	Enable performance-impacting dtrace probes.	Yes	No
-XX:-AllowUserSignal Handlers	Do not complain if the application installs signal handlers.	Yes	Yes
-XX:ThreadStack Size=512	Thread stack size (in Kbytes). (Zero means use default stack size) [Sparc: 512; Solaris x86: 320 (was 256 prior in 5.0 and earlier); Sparc 64 bit: 1024; Linux amd64: 1024 (was zero in 5.0 and earlier); all others zero.]	Yes	Yes

7.3.4.2 Migrating from Solaris to Linux

Attribute	Impact
-XX:+UseLargePages	On Solaris, the UseLargePages flag is selected by default. It needs to be turned on in Linux, as using large pages improves performance.
	When you migrate your Java application to Linux use these settings:
	Set the -XX:+UseLargePages at the JVM level for Sun HotSpot.
	On IBM JVM it is -Xlp, and JRockit - XXlargePages. Set the huge pages at OS level. Refer to *How to enable Large pages in Windows and Linux*: http://www.vmware.com/files/pdf/large_pg_performance

7.3.4.2 Migrating from 32-bit JVM to 64-bit JVM

Often, migrating from UNIX to Linux may present an opportunity to also upgrade from a 32-bit to 64-bit JVM, but there are a few considerations to keep in mind. It is not mandatory to upgrade to a 64-bit JVM to use a 64-bit OS, but it is a good practice if you are able to do so.

Attribute	Impact
Memory Size	You need to load test your application, Refer to the *Chapter on Design and Sizing Enterprise Java on VMware* for design and sizing guidelines.
	Memory utilization of the same application within a 32-bit architecture will likely use more heap space as a result of 64-bit object representation. Therefore keep the following in mind:
	• You may need to retune your heap space setting to new values that you determine by doing load testing. Values such -Xms and −Xmx need to be adjusted to accommodate the increase in internal-object and types representation of 64-bit JVM.
	• You potentially need to readjust your GC settings.
	The benefits of going to a 64-bit JVM and OS include the ability to use larger maximum heap settings. Many of the 32-bit limitations, such as the 1.54GB to 3.8GB heap limitation (depending which OS you were using) are removed, and 64-bit heap sizes can be much larger. We see VMware customers with 12GB heap sizes. Very large heap sizes come with the need to tune your GC. For tuning guidelines refer to your JVM vendor's documentation.
	Increased pointer-addressing size in the 64-bit JVMs means that an application might have run fine within, for example, 1GB RAM/Heap 32-bit JVM. But you may now find under 64-bit JVM that it needs at least 2GB memory. To mitigate the effect of increased address space due to 64 bit addressing, you can use XX:+UseCompressedOops. This will treat the address space as 32-bit, hence saving on lots of memory space even though it is in 64-bit JVM. The only limitation is that this can only be used with JVM heap size of up to 32GB.

7.4 FAQ: Migrating from Physical to Virtual

"With UNIX-based hardware I have very large machines running all of my Java applications. What should be my migration-sizing strategy, and what are the VMware vSphere maximums that I need to be aware of?"

One of the most important steps is to conduct a load test that will help you determine the ideal individual-VM size and how many JVMs you can stack up (vertical scalability). Based on this repeatable building-block *VM*, scale-out to determine what is best for your application traffic profile.

It helps to know the VMware vSphere maximums. For information, see Configuration Maximums: VMware vSphere 4.1: http://www. vmware.com/pdf/vsphere4/r41/vsp_41_config_max.pdf, NOTE: the maximums below are for VMware vSphere 4.1, and it is anticipated these will be changed in future releases. Always refer to configuration maximums on the VMware site as to the latest maximums. But suffice to say that as of the writing of this book, the maximums quoted here are current for vSphere 4.1. The most notable changes within vSphere5 will be the ability to create up to 32vCPU VMs, and memory usage of up to 1TB. Also unique to vSphere5 is the fact that the NUMA architecture will be exposed to the Guest OS so that some very large database type of workloads could take advantage of it. In vSphere4.1 as mentioned earlier the NUMA architecture details are not exposed to the Guest OS, in the case of Java this shouldn't matter whether you are using vSphere4.1 or vSphere5, the NUMA locality of staying within 2vCPU, 4vCPU, and 8vCPU (assuming the hardware used has NUMA nodes that are that wide) then you are already using ESX scheduler NUMA optimizations without any need for further tuning. You will also not need turn on the -XX:UseNUMA option on the JVM since the ESX scheduler NUMA optimizations are highly effective. If you suspect that you have a NUMA locality problem you can inspect the esxtop parameter N%L, if this is below 100% then your VMs are not NUMA local and you would need to size in accordance of the memory available to your NUMA nodes, along with sizing vCPU within the available cores per socket/NUMA node.

Table 5 below for some important maximums in vSphere 4.1.

Table 5 *vSphere 4.1 Configuration Maximum*

vSphere Configuration	Maximum
Per VM	8-vCPUs
	255GB
	2TB of storage minus 512bytes
Per Host	512-vCPUs
	320 VMs
	25 vCPUs per core
Per vCenter	1,000 hosts
	10,000 powered on VMs
	15,000 registered VMs
	10 linked vCenter Servers
	3,000 hosts in linked vCenter servers
	30,000 powered on VMs in linked vCenter Servers
	50,000 registered VMs in linked vCenter Servers
	100 concurrent vSphere Clients
	400 hosts per datacenter

"What are new decisions that must be made for applications running on virtual that we did not have to make for native environments?"

You have to determine the optimal size of the repeatable building-block VM. Establish this by benchmarking, along with total scale-out factor. Determine how many concurrent users each single vCPU configuration of your application can handle, and then extrapolate that to your production traffic to determine overall compute-resource requirements for vCPU, memory, storage, and network. Having a symmetrical building block (for example, every VM having the same number of vCPUs), helps keep load distribution even from your load balancer. The benchmarking tests help you determine how large a single VM should be (vertical scalability) and how many VMs you will need (horizontal scalability).

You need to pay special attention to scale-out factor and see up to what point it is linear within your application running on top of VMware. Enterprise Java applications are multi-tiered, and bottlenecks can occur at any point along the scale-out performance line and quickly cause non-linear results. The assumption of linear scalability may not always be true, and it is essential to load test a preproduction replica (production to be) of your environment to accurately size for you traffic.

"I have conducted extensive GC sizing and tuning for our current enterprise Java application running on physical. Do I have to adjust any sizing when moving this Java application to virtualized environment?"

No. All tuning that you perform for your Java application on physical is transferrable to your virtual environment. However, because virtualization projects are typically about driving a high-consolidation ratio, it is advisable that you follow the guidelines in *Design and Sizing Enterprise Java on VMware Chapter* to establish the ideal compute-resource configuration for your individual VMs, the number of JVMs within a VM, and the overall number of VMs on the ESX/ESXi host.

Additionally, because this type of migration involves an OS/platform change along with JVM vendor change, it is advisable to review the chapter, along with your vendor's tuning advice for both OS and JVM.

The GC tuning that you would have done would predominantly fall into two overall categories. Either you tuned for throughput or for response time. The throughput type of GC collectors are geared to give you better overall throughput, and gencon type of GCs are geared towards giving you better response time. For example, enterprise Java Web applications may benefit from gencon policy, while perhaps job scheduler/batch type of Java applications will benefit from throughput collector.

"How many and what size of virtual machines will I need?"

This depends on the nature of your application. However, most often the 2-vCPU VMs are common building blocks for Java applications. One of the guidelines is to tune your system for more scale-out as opposed to scale-up. This is not an inflexible rule, as it depends on your organization's architectural best practices. Smaller, more scaled-out VMs may provide better overall architecture. But you incur additional guest-OS licensing costs. If this is a constraint, you can tune towards larger 4-vCPU VMs and stack more JVMs on it.

"What is the correct number of JVMs per virtual machine?"

There is no one definitive answer, as this largely depends on the nature of your application. The benchmarking you conduct can reveal the limit of the number of JVMs you can stack up on a single VM.

The more JVMs you put on a single VM, the more JVM overhead and cost is incurred when initializing a JVM. Alternately, instead of stacking up multiple JVMs within a VM, you can increase the JVM size vertically by adding more threads and heap size. This can be achieved if your JVM is within an application server such as Tomcat. So instead of increasing the number of JVMs, you can increase the number of concurrent threads available and resources that a single Tomcat JVM can service for your n-number of applications deployed and their concurrent requests per second. The limitation of how many applications you can stack up within a single application-server instance/JVM is bounded by how large you can afford your JVM heap size to be and by performance impact. A very large JVM heap size beyond 4GB needs to be tested for performance and GC cycle impact, and the trade-offs need to be examined. This concern is not specific to virtualization—it equally applies to physical-server setup.

7.5 References

- *Guidelines: UNIX to Linux Novell Migration Tools: Novell Migration Tools* at http://www.novell.com/developer/porting_and_migration_tools.html
- UNIX-to-Linux IBM Migration Guide

- IBM Linux center: http://www.ibm.com/developerworks/linux/
- Linux migration tools: http://www.ibm.com/developerworks/linux/library/l-roadmap.html
- IBM assessment paper: http://www.ibm.com/developerworks/linux/library/l-solar/
- IBM guide http://www.redbooks.ibm.com/redbooks/pdfs/sg247186.pdf
- UNIX to Linux RedHat Migration Tools: *Red Hat Migration center* page at http://www.redhat.com/migrate/rhel_overview/
- Best Practices for Running Java in a Virtual Machine: http://www.vmware.com/resources/techresources/1087

Chapter 8

Run Effectively in Production

8.1 Overview

Running in production involves having many processes down to a repeatable science. This is especially true for enterprise Java applications, as the majority tend to be custom-developed in-house applications that have a development, deployment, and runtime lifecycles. In this chapter we briefly delve into the best practices for each of these steps of the enterprise Java development, deployment, and runtime processes.

8.2 Development Best Practices

While there are many Java-development best practices out there in terms of the "how to code" category, I won't attempt to delve into this, as I believe there is more than adequate set of mindshare out there. I will instead focus on some of the complementary best practices that have worked for me from the experience of writing Java code for the last fifteen years.

- ***Maintain good version-control, unit-test, and regression libraries***:
  - ○ ***Version control***:-
    - ▪ This goes without saying, but for completeness I have found this can be half-baked at times, as code check-ins by developers are too relaxed. Anyone can check into the developer branch, and perhaps he or she should.
    - ▪ Forcing all developers to often check out of the main developer branch and integrate the latest branch

changes into their code as often as possible has prov-en to improve the development process.

- However, developer code check-ins tends to happen without much control. Sure, any developer can check into the developer branch. Some have opted into hav-ing one branch per developer, and then a main devel-oper trunk branch. Regardless, this developer main trunk still needs to be adhered to by all developers, and often. Otherwise, all the developer branches will be digressing to a point where it becomes literally im-possible to keep things coherently integrated.
- A good practice is to have one main developer branch or trunk that all developers must check out from, and often, but also must check into when they are ready. However, they should only do so once they have run a unit-test or regression-test library that checks their code prior to being checked in.
- This regression library is designed to prevent the "about to be checked-in code" from causing serious errors to the main developer branch, which may immediately affect other developers if they were to check out from the developer main branch. It is a foreign concept, I have found, to many developers that they are being forced to run a set of regression scripts every time they needed to check in. However, with time they have grown to love it. This simple step saves you many wast-ed cycles, often due to code that should not have made it into the developer branch. This is not to be confused with an integration test ranch. You could think of the main developer branch as a pre-integration testing branch, from which the full-code integration branch can be built, and then from which a QA branch and prod branches can be built.

- ***Regression-libraries and unit-test libraries as test ware***: The point made above about forcing the successful run of a regression-test library run prior to developer code check-in implies that a decent regression library is well maintained by a team that ideally is independent of the development team. As developers create software, there are other developers creating test ware, which has similar code-management constraints as regular software development in terms of upkeep and making sure it has the latest and greatest business logic.
- ***Nightly builds, regression, code-coverage reports***: While assuming developers have done due diligence, it is important to create a report of the code segments that were changed during developer check-ins for the day, and these should be made available for all developers, ideally as part of a peer-review process. The nightly process should also run coverage reports and regression functional tests, and report to the developer any test cases that might have failed.

8.3 Deployment Best Practices

The notion of deployment here implies preparing the Java custom code to be pushed from development branches to staging and integration branches, and then onto further QA branches, and then ultimately to production.

Having established good regression libraries and nightly build process, the QA and/or release engineering team can rely on understanding the development process better and have a certain level of confidence to go about producing new builds upon which QA can test.

Here are some key best practices:

- ***Always use a scripted approach***. I continue to like Ant for its power and ease of use. Also, scripts written in Ant are cross-platform; they essentially run as a Java application. You saw in Chapter 5 that you can have one master Ant script that is able to marshal all of the deployment pieces, including the following: build, create, and deploy Java-code war files/ear files, execute any SQL scripts, interact with load-balancer scripts if need be, and be able to create virtual-machines templates and/or virtual machines during the deployment process.

- **Use VMs and VM templates**. Creating VM machines for temporary use is a key requirement for building an environment quickly in QA. Also, saving these VMs as templates helps speed up future deployments, along with keeping consistency across builds.
- **Conduct a load test and take thread dumps**. No doubt this topic has been well addressed in chapter 4, but conducting a vertical scalability (establish building-block VM) and horizontal scalability is important. But it is worthy to highlight that when the load reaches the peak, it is important to take a thread dump of the Java application and inspect the thread dump for any threads that may be in a locked state. A conversation between the performance engineers and the developers should be started to help resolve this. Thread-lock problems are notorious scalability and high-availability inhibitors.

8.4 Runtime Best Practices

This section is all about being effective in running enterprise Java applications in production in such a way that you are meeting your SLAs. Some of the points below no doubt we have covered throughout the book, but lets summarize.

Key best practices for running enterprise Java applications in production:

- **Use synthetic transactions**. This measures response time. Particularly if your application is geographically distributed, then where the synthetic transactions are run is pretty imperative to give you the right response time. The synthetic transaction should exercise a sufficient portion of the enterprise Java application stack, but without causing a huge burden on the execution of the regular real-user transactions. Many times I find the use of the account-login function as the most common synthetic transaction that is used to keep track of application response time. There are multiple ways you can set this up. You can choose to do it yourself via scripting (for example, set up a synthetic transaction via a script that runs from the load-balancer layer), or you can simply buy a service from various providers like WebsitePulse and SiteUpTime, to name a couple.

- **Additional monitoring**. Now to cover this topic holistically, a whole book would be needed. But suffice to say, choosing a good monitoring tool, and one that is able to interact with virtualization, is well worth it. I personally rely on esxtop and vCenter charts, and I have grown to like products like Zenoss for monitoring both virtual and non-virtual systems. For additional application-level monitoring tools, Spring Insight and Hyperic are also very useful in being able to drill down to the source of the problem.

- **Conduct postmortems**. It is important whenever there is a problem in production that the entire stack should be analyzed, and logs at each level must be collected, from both physical and virtual (esxtop and/or vCenter charts), along with typical sar reports. But in addition to this, and specifically for Java applications, a Java thread dump should always be taken before any restart of JVM action is conducted. These logs, along with the thread dump, reveal code secrets not known to many, which you can then, in concert with a developer, be able to analyze the hot spots in the code that are scalability and performance inhibiters. I used many forms of taking a Java thread dump and thread-analysis tools (for example, Samurai). You can refer to Chapter 11 for details.

- **Deployment certification**. Only accept application code into production after you have seen the performance test, associated thread dumps, code-inspection or code-review report, and the regression-test report. If any of these are missing, you are basically at the mercy of those notorious three lines of Java code that can undo any production-quality built infrastructure. I continually see infrastructure departments of IT hiring more and more professionals with IT applications-development backgrounds to simply combat these kind of scenarios.

Chapter 9

Performance Study

9.1 Introduction

There are several Java on vSphere performance studies that are public. Highlighted in this chapter is a very useful performance study conducted by Harold Rosenberg, senior performance engineer at VMware.

The full performance paper is a public document available here: http://www.vmware.com/resources/techresources/10158

9.2 Olio Architecture Setup

In Figure 39 the left side of the diagram you have the Geo-coders that drive load towards the application VMs, along with an NFS file store where images are stored. The application places a lot of traffic onto the network, and it is geared around demonstrating how the network would likely become a bottleneck before the VMware stack would.

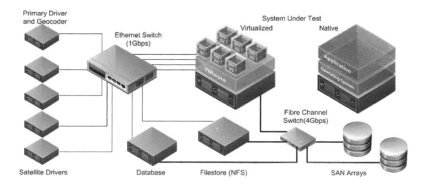

Figure 39: *Shows the Olio test setup*

9.3 Looking at the Results

In the ninetieth percentile case, the response-time curves and CPU utilizations for the 2CPU native and virtualized cases are shown. Below 80 percent CPU utilization in the VM, the native and virtual configurations have essentially identical performance, with only minimal absolute differences in response times.

9.3.1 Native 2-CPU vs. Virtual 2-vCPU

This section shows the results for the 2CPU native/physical server versus a 2-vCPU VM. Plotted in Figure 40 is the response time (R/T) and CPU utilization. The graph clearly shows that at 80 percent CPU utilization, a threshold is reached. For the response time up to 80 percent, the response time matches that of the physical-server case, and beyond the 80 percent threshold there is slight divergence, although still within a reasonable difference. As for the CPU utilization, we see the numbers compare quite well with each other.

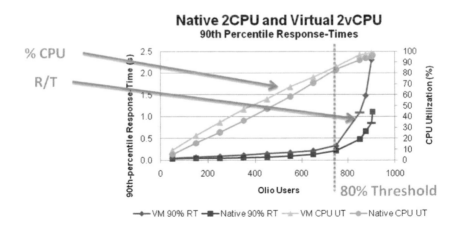

Figure 40: *Shows native 2CPU versus virtual 2-vCPU*

9.3.2 Native 4CPU versus Virtual 4-vCPU

This section shows the results for the 4CPU native/Physical server, vs. a 4vCPU VM. Plotted in Figure 41 is the Response Time (R/T) and CPU utilization. The graph clearly shows that at 80% CPU utilization there a threshold is reached. For the response time up to the 80% the response time matches that of the physical server case, and beyond the 80% threshold there is slight divergence although still within a reasonable difference. As for the CPU utilization, we see the numbers compare quite well with each other.

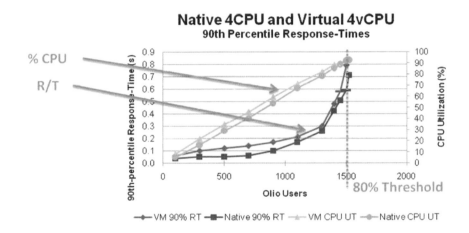

Figure 41: *Shows native 4CPU versus virtual 4-vCPU*

9.3.3 Peak Throughput by CPU Count

In Figure 42 shown for the 1CPU case, native was able to achieve ninety-five ops/sec versus eighty-five ops/sec for virtual (10.5 percent difference). In the 2CPU case, it was 179 ops/sec for native versus 169 ops/sec for virtual (5.5.percent difference). In the 4CPU case, it was 298 ops/sec for native versus 193 ops/sec for virtual (1.67 percent difference). This shows that as the CPU was increased, the throughput tracked well and closer to the native case.

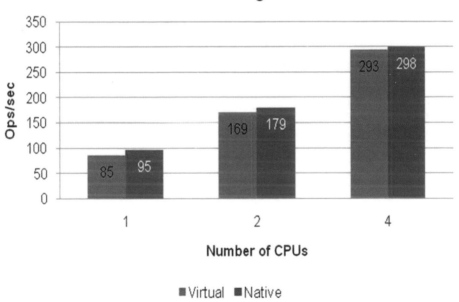

Figure 42: *Shows ops/sec versus number of CPUs as a measure of throughput*

9.3.4 Comparing 1-vCPU to 4-vCPU Configuration Choices

In Figure 43 , the three configurations shown are made of four VMs with 1-vCPU each, two VMs with 2-vCPU each, and one VM of 4-vCPU. The graph has a ninetieth-percentile response time on the left vertical axis, CPU utilization on the right vertical axis, and the number of users on the horizontal axis. We see that the 2-vCPU configuration leads the best-of-breed combination user throughput for the least amount of heap memory at a total of 5G across two VMs, or 2.5GB per 2-vCPU VM.

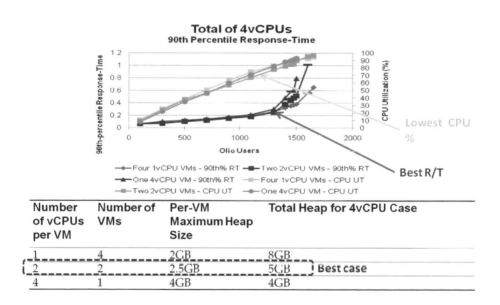

Number of vCPUs per VM	Number of VMs	Per-VM Maximum Heap Size	Total Heap for 4vCPU Case	
1	4	2GB	8GB	
2	2	2.5GB	5GB	Best case
4	1	4GB	4GB	

Figure 43: *Shows three configuration choices ranging from four off 1-vCPU, two off 2-vCPU VMs and one off 4-vCPU VM*

In Figure 44 we illustrate the peak throughput of the four 1vCPU VMs, 2 off 2 vCPU VMs, and 1 off 4 vCPU VM. Again clearly demonstrated is that the 2 off 2 vCPU case is the best throughput. Now the reason why this is chosen as the best result ahead of the 1 vCPU VMs is because for any serious production applications 2 vCPU VMs are what is most commonly used. If you have a Java application that is fairly busy, then you can expect the GC to occupy one vCPU, and the second vCPU would be made available for regular user transactions. If on the other hand you had 1vCPU VM then GC and regular user transactions would be contending for CPU cycles.

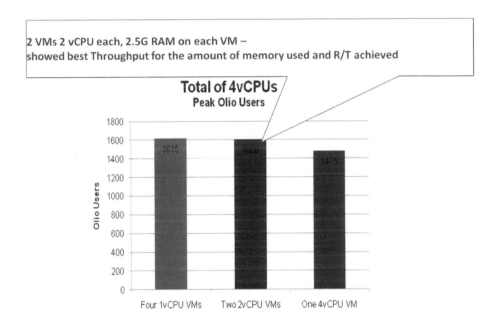

Figure 44: *Shows peak Olio users versus various VM vCPU configurations*

Chapter 10

Application Modernization and vFabric

10.1 Introduction

VMware's vFabric is a cloud-application platform made of various components, as shown in Figure 45, where we show the main components that are part of vFabric.

As you can see from various chapters we have covered in this book, a lot of issues dealt with Virtualizing your applications as is, without any changes. However, there comes a point where you feel that the underlying application architecture of your application needs to be revamped and modernized in a way that can handle the new scale of your business. Whether this is the data and associated data objects, common design patterns and framework, messaging, batch frameworks, monitoring, or the runtime container - all of these at some point may prove to be challenging your SLAs. Any of the highly robust vFabric components can be used to address these architectural concerns within your application.

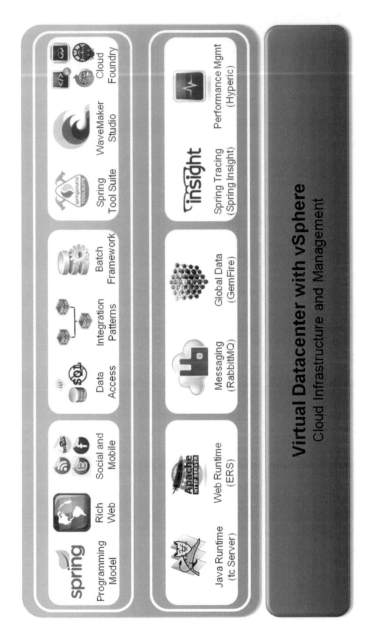

Figure 45: *Shows VMware vFabric, a cloud-application platform that sits on top of VMware cloud infrastructure and management layer.*

In the next section we look at each one of the components that make up the vFabric platform.

10.2 Programming Models and the Spring Framework

Naturally, the Spring framework has proliferated among the Java-development community in the last seven years and has become a de facto enterprise Java-development framework. Largely, vFabric is geared around developer productivity. Spring Framework is a topic worthy of a whole book, so we won't attempt to re-create the wheel here, and suffice to say that other authors have sufficiently covered the Spring Framework and SpringIOC/Dependency Injection topic.

10.3 Spring Rich Web

As illustrated in Figure 46 the foundation of the Spring Rich Web set of modules is built around the Spring Web MVC module, with three other modules: Spring Faces, Spring Web Flow, and Spring JavaScript.

- Spring Web Flow framework is a component of the Spring Rich Web Modules that is focused on the definition and execution of UI flow within a web application. The system allows you to capture a logical flow of your Web application as a self-contained module that can be reused in different situations. Such a flow guides a single user through the implementation of a business task, and represents a single user execution. Flows often execute across HTTP requests, have state, exhibit transactional characteristics, and may be dynamic and/or long-running in nature.
- Spring JavaScript provides Ajax support as a lightweight abstraction over common JavaScript toolkits.
- Spring Faces is the home of the Spring Web Flow + JSF integration layer, as well as a number of additional value adds specific to a JSF environment. These value adds include the following:
    o Unified EL Integration, which is a separate implementation of the ExpressionParser from Spring Binding that uses the new Unified EL from JSF 1.2 and JSP 2.1.

Both JSF 1.1 and 1.2 implementations are provided. This allows for JSF users to use the same expression language in their flow definitions as in their JSF views, and to have access to the full chain of JSF resolvers for expression evaluation.

o Client Side Validation Components, which is a small set of JSF components that work as "advisors" on regular JSF inputText components. These components make use of the rich validation capabilities of the Ext JavaScript framework.

Figure 46: *Shows the components of the Spring Rich Web modules*

10.4 Social and Mobile

Spring Social is an extension of the Spring Framework that allows you to connect your applications with software-as-a-service (SaaS) providers such as Facebook and Twitter.

- An extensible service-provider framework that greatly simplifies the process of connecting local user accounts to hosted provider accounts.
- A connect controller that handles the authorization flow between your Java or Spring Web application, a service provider, and your users.
- Java bindings to popular service0provider APIs such as Facebook, Twitter, LinkedIn, TripIt, GitHub, and Gowalla.
- Sign-in controllers that enable users to authenticate with your application by signing in to Facebook or Twitter.

10.5 Data Access and the Spring Data Module

The primary goal of the Spring Data project is to make it easier to build Spring-powered applications that use new data-access technologies such as non-relational databases, map-reduce frameworks, and cloud-based data services, as well as provide improved support for relational database technologies. NoSQL-type of data stores fall into the following categories:

- Blob stores, such as Amazon S3, Rackspace, and Azure.
- Column stores, such as HBase and Cassandra
- Document stores, such as CouchDB, MongoDb, and Neo4j
- Graph databases, such as Neo4j
- Key value stores, such as Riak, Redis, and Membase
- Map-reduce, such as Hadoop
- RDBMS, such as JDBC extensions, JPA

You can find additional information on the Spring Data project here: www.springsource.org/spring-data

10.6 Integration Patterns

Spring Integration provides an extension of the Spring programming model to support the well-known Enterprise Integration Patterns (refer to http://www.eaipatterns.com/). It enables lightweight messaging within Spring-based applications and supports integration with external systems via declarative adapters. Those adapters provide a higher-level of abstraction over Spring's support for remoting, messaging, and scheduling. Spring Integration's primary goal is to provide a simple model for building enterprise-integration solutions while maintaining the separation of concerns that is essential for producing maintainable, testable code.

10.7 Batch Framework

Batch processing continues to be a large part of enterprise applications, and while it is a legacy pattern, it is one of the most useful ones in fulfilling critical business functions. Spring Batch is a lightweight, comprehensive batch framework designed to enable the development of robust batch applications vital for the daily operations of enterprise systems. Spring Batch builds upon the productivity, POJO-based development approach and the general ease-of-use capabilities people have come to know from the Spring Framework, while making it easy for developers to access and leverage more advanced enterprise services when necessary.

10.8 Spring ToolSuite

SpringSource Tool Suite™ (STS) provides the best Eclipse-powered development environment for building Spring-powered enterprise applications. STS supplies tools for all of the latest enterprise Java-, Spring-, Groovy-, and Grails-based technologies, as well as the most advanced tooling available for enterprise OSGi development. Included with STS is the developer edition of vFabric tc Server, the drop-in replacement for Apache Tomcat that's optimized for Spring. With its Spring Insight console, tc Server Developer Edition (refer to http://www.springsource.com/developer/tcserver), this provides a graphical real-time view of application-performance metrics that lets developers identify and diagnose problems from their desktops. STS supports application targeting to local, virtual, and cloud-based servers. It is freely available for development and internal business-operations use with no time limits.

10.9 WaveMaker

WaveMaker is a rapid application-development environment for building, maintaining, and modernizing business-critical Web 2.0 applications. It eliminates Java coding for building Web 2.0 applications, allowing developers to focus on solving business problems. It uses a WYSIWYG approach to development, and it generates standard Java apps that are extensible.

10.10 CloudFoundry

CloudFoundry is the project initiated by VMware that features an open platform as a service. It can support multiple frameworks, multiple cloud providers, and multiple application services, all on a cloud-scale platform.

Developer productivity: Build applications with your choice of high-productivity frameworks and application services.

Open system: Choose your framework, choose your cloud, or choose your application services.

Faster delivery: Shorten the time it takes to move your application from concept, to code, to the cloud, using an open platform as a service.

10.11 tc Server

This is an Apache Tomcat-based servlet container that you can deploy and run Web application war files on. VMware has three editions that are described below. One of the benefits of using this is the highly performing jdbc pool (see: http://people.apache.org/~fhanik/jdbc-pool/jdbc-pool.html). Refer to Table 6 for further description of the features within each edition.

Table 6: *tc Server Editions*

Feature	Developer Edition	Standard Edition	Spring Edition
Apache Tomcat compatible	√	√	√
Multiserver configuration		√	√
Secure remote-server administration		√	√
Command line control and scripting		√	√
Comprehensive integrated monitoring		√	√

Feature	Developer Edition	Standard Edition	Spring Edition
Spring application control (start/stop/restart)	√	√	√
Native Spring instrumentation	√		√
Detailed Spring app-performance reporting	√		√
Thread tracing and response-time analysis	√		√
Integrated into SpringSource Tool Suite	√		

10.12 ERS

With VMware vFabric Enterprise Ready Server (ERS) you get enterprise-level performance, scalability, and security, while reducing the cost and complexity of sophisticated Web infrastructures. ERS is the Web server and load-balancing component based on the most widely distributed Apache Web server package.

10.13 RabbitMQ

RabbitMQ is a messaging product that can be used on enterprise applications. It is an open-source project, and you can read full details here: http://www.rabbitmq.com/documentation.html.

It is based on the AMQP, which is the open standard for business messaging, and through various adapters it can support SMPTP, STOMP, and HTTP for lightweight Web messaging.

You can use RabbitMQ to achieve enterprise application-implementation patterns, such as the following:

- Worker queues for distributing work amongst various workers
- Publish/subscribe mechanisms for sending a message to many consumers at the same time

- Routing patterns for receiving filtered or routed messages
- Topic patterns for receiving messages based on a pattern
- RPC calls for remote procedure calls

10.14 Spring Insight

Spring Insight is a technology that gives you visibility into your application's runtime performance and behavior.

- See the SQL executed for any page request
- Find pages that are executing slowly and drill into the cause
- Verify that your application's transactions are working as designed

10.15 Hyperic

Find, fix, and prevent performance problems in custom Web applications, whether running on a physical, virtual, or cloud infrastructure. With its ability to continuously monitor fifty thousand metrics across seventy-five Web technologies, refer to: http://www.vmware.com/products/datacenter-virtualization/vfabric-hyperic/plugins.html. Hyperic provides sysadmins the deep visibility they need to ensure server performance, reduce downtime, and meet SLAs. Hyperic automatically discovers new virtual machines as they come online, eliminating the need for manual updating of monitoring configurations.

- Detect and resolve performance issues before users even notice
- Gain complete visibility into your application infrastructure
- Configure server monitoring in minutes

10.16 VMware vFabric GemFire

Since the vFabric GemFire component plays a critical role regarding data in the cloud, this section takes a detailed architectural perspective of the distributed data systems.

This section looks at the critical role of application data to the successful running of highly scalable and available enterprise Java applications. We briefly examine the history of relational data and its growth over the past few decades as a main data store for enterprise applications, and we look at how this design paradigm is quickly changing to adapt to both existing and newer applications. In most cases, the adoption is a rapid response to an ever-increasing demand of having faster response times, higher availability, better scalability, and cost-efficient manageability. Internet growth has made it easier to reach end users from anywhere around the globe, and this wide proliferation has added new challenges for enterprise applications. These challenges can only be met by improving some legacy aspects of data's role in application architectures. In-memory distributed data management systems (IDDM systems) such as VMware vFabric™ GemFire provide solutions for many of the challenges of traditional databases.

10.16.1 Application Data Background

Enterprise Java applications rely heavily on application data stored in relational databases. With this comes an increased cost of maintaining and scaling these databases to meet the growing demand from users. Partly, this complexity is rooted in the history of relational databases, as they were designed as large, singular silos where all application data is stored on disk, and as a result the only scalability option is to scale vertically. As a result of the vertical-scalability approach, the purchase of a faster and more powerful server is needed every time capacity limits are reached, and this always proved to be not the most cost effective way.

The singular-silo-database limitation also created an interesting challenge for enterprise Java application architects seeking to reach wider audiences geographically. Either fulfill application requests for data travel over a wide geographic area to the large master database and suffer the resulting latency in response time, or create a local, replicated database instance. A local database improves response time, but it needs fast replication to synchronize with the master database. With database replication there is additional complexity (for example, the time window needed for replication, and whether it can be done seamlessly while keeping data consistency across all database instances). To some extent this scalability limitation of singular-silo databases was mitigated by having inter-database synchronization/ replication technology, and recently some relational databases have added clustering technologies. However, with these replication and clustering features come added cost and complexity, and they still do not fulfill the rigorous requirements of modern enterprise Java applications.

In many cases, enterprise Java Web application requirements for fast transactional response times are typically to be less than one second, and are on the order of milliseconds for Java middleware applications. If response times exceed these processing time limits, users quickly complain about the performance of the application. However, if in a typical enterprise Java application you have to constantly hop an additional network node to go to the database to get information for the enterprise Java application data, meeting the one-second response time is quite challenging. Alternatives such as in memory caching and in memory data need to be considered.

Since the 1970s, when they were first introduced as a technology, relational databases have had a significant positive impact on how application functionality can be delivered to end users. However, a lot of the design and implementation assumptions for relational databases are based on data living on a storage disk, and an excessive amount of locking is used to ensure concurrency control. Because of this legacy-design attribute, relational databases do not naturally scale horizontally. Enterprise Java applications are simpler to scale horizontally through load-balancer and application-server clustering. This natural design impedance, having one application tier able to easily scale-out horizontally to meet demand dynamically, while the other application tier has to scale vertically (in this case, the database tier), adds increasing complexity for architects trying to keep abreast of enterprise Java application SLAs.

Figure 47 illustrates aspects of relational databases in a classical enterprise Java application. Though relational databases scale up vertically, they don't necessarily scale horizontally in a cost-effective manner. Compounding the horizontal-scalability limitation is the need for applications to cross another network hop to get data, resulting in slower transaction response times. Clearly there is architectural design impedance between the horizontal scale-out approach of the Java middle tier, and the vertical scale-up story of relational databases. Horizontal scaling using x86 commodity hardware with virtualization is more cost effective than a vertical-scalability approach.

Since the mass adoption of relational databases in the last twenty years, there has been significant shift in the cost of hardware and, in particular, the cost of memory. More data can be kept in memory in a cost-effective manner.

Complementing relational databases with a layer such as an IDDM can significantly improve their architectural worthiness for today's rigorous requirements for fast response time, scalability, and availability.

IDDM systems add the horizontal-scalability feature to the data-scalability story that more closely matches the scalability approach of the Java applications.

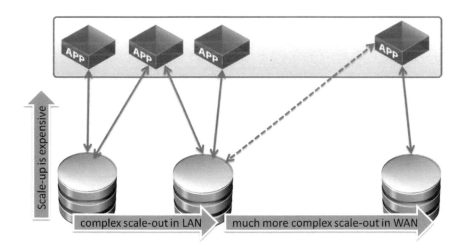

Figure 47: *Shows a traditional enterprise application with relational database*

10.16.2 Emerging Trends

Thus far we have looked at the challenges of traditional relational data roles within enterprise applications, and discussed how an IDDM system can be used to mitigate some of the challenges. In this section we discuss what the trends of IDDM system proliferation are, and what types of applications can benefit from these features.

With the wide proliferation of commodity hardware and significantly reduced memory (RAM) prices, IDDM systems are becoming a core part of architectures that drive modern enterprise applications. In particular, applications that have high requirements for rapid response time, less than a one-second range for Java Web applications and in milliseconds for enterprise Java middleware systems, are now using IDDM systems in production to effectively guard against traditional relational database failures.

Though having this data in memory helps to speed up data discovery, an additional mechanism that speeds up data discovery is warranted. VMware vFabric GemFire supports fast-distributed data discovery by installing the partitioning algorithm on each machine (code) including (optionally) clients. The partitioning metadata is distributed to all nodes, so the data-discovery function is executed in parallel across many nodes.

> *NOTE:* Data-gathering functions can be executed on just one node, executed in parallel on a subset of nodes, or in parallel across all nodes. This programming model is referred to as map-reduce, where users can specify a map function that processes a key/value pair to generate a set of intermediate key/value pairs, and an associated reduce function that merges all intermediate associated values with the same intermediate key to yield the final data set requested by the data-gathering function. Because the main notion is to split up the execution of getting many pieces of data across many nodes of commodity hardware, speed of execution is vastly increased.

10.16.3 Map-reduce Implementations

Though many map-reduce implementations have recently been popularized, VMware vFabric GemFire offers a production-proven technology that has been demonstrated to work on financial-transaction systems that have zero tolerance for transactional failure, and many other mission-critical examples from other industries. Complementing GemFire are other vFabric modules that help implement a highly scalable distributed application rapidly within one framework, the VMware foundation for the cloud-application platform known collectively as vFabric. The framework covers all aspects of development, through to runtime deployment concerns of a highly scalable distributed application. Unlike its open-source counterparts, vFabric is fully supported.

10.16.4 Highly Scalable and Available Data with IDDM Systems

The background of application data poses challenges to architects designing highly scalable and available enterprise Java applications. But each of the design impedances of relational databases can be mitigated by an IDDM system feature, and this paves the way for a new approach, where data lives architecturally in modern enterprise Java applications.

IDDM systems specifically address necessary features for distributed enterprise Java applications, such as horizontal scalability, regional data distribution and data edging, grouping of data from multiple data sources, various distribution models for communication between members of the distributed system, flexibility of various configurations that can be changed without contention, failure detection, and replication.

There has been an increase in adoption of IDDM systems in the last few years due to recent popularization of the map-reduce parallel-execution programming model that is currently being used by several large implementations. The map-reduce model allows the execution of application data-gathering functions on one Java virtual machine (JVM), or executed in parallel on several nominated JVMs, or on all JVM members that are comprised in the IDDM system.

10.16.5 IDDM Systems Horizontal Scalability

One of the greatest challenges is that while enterprise Java application platforms scale very well horizontally, the relational databases systems tier doesn't. Considering that enterprise Java applications are highly distributed, whether they are running across multiple tiers and across multiple geographic regions, a complementary distributed-data system can be used to enhance the applications horizontal scalability. In this regard, an IDDM system is an effective way of adding horizontally scalable data, so that as you scale out your enterprise Java application, the data distribution scales accordingly in near linear fashion. IDDM systems achieve this horizontal scalability by allowing you to add new JVM instances, along with the enterprise Java application they host, dynamically, with minimal effort. These new JVM instances immediately start servicing data in whatever view of the data has been configured in them, to all of the other JVM instances that are part of the distributed data system. Essentially a distributed data system is an in-memory database that is tuned to have only the data that your application needs available to it.

10.16.6 Regional Data Distribution and Data Edging with IDDM Systems

An IDDM system must be able to distribute the data to quickly service the application context so that the data that an application needs in one region is co-located nearby (edging the data nearer to its intended transactional use) so that the transactional response time is optimal. An IDDM system is essentially a network of coordinated JVM application nodes that share data across many regions in order to fulfill an application request for data. Modern IDDM systems can offer data distribution across a cluster of nodes, providing a choice of full replication to selected application nodes, or a fault-tolerant partition of data across selected nodes. Some IDDM systems may chose to log every data update to disk, but more advanced implementations that are tuned for better performance use their fault-tolerance mechanism to apply a replica of the update to one or more node in the IDDM system.

10.16.7 Grouping and Data Coalescing from Multiple Relational Data Stores with IDDM Systems

IDDM systems also offer the ability to group data from various regions. A region can be a small set or a very large number of data objects. These groups can be shared among millions of transactions, if needed. An example could be a static product list that can be updated on a periodic basis. Additionally, IDDM systems can have multiple Java-applications instances distributed across multiple regions, all having the ability to access multiple traditional relational databases. Regardless of their geographic region, they appear to be one consistent data set across your entire enterprise Java application. IDDM systems are able to manage transactional data consistency at the application layer through various configuration mechanisms.

10.16.8 Multiple Distribution Models with IDDM Systems

When dealing with distributed systems such as an advanced implementation IDDM system, there are three distribution models:

- Peer-to-Peer (P2P): All members have direct connectivity to each other. This is mostly applicable to the case where application logic is running locally and is a long-lived process, with cached data on a set of server nodes. This is also known as process-to-data affinity. In this case, too many short-lived processes would probably overwhelm the IDDM system.
- Client Server: Client-application processes connect and load balance across a subset of P2P IDDM servers. Each client may employ data edging if needed to improve response time performance. The client-server configuration is mostly applicable for applications that require thousands of connections to the server, such as computational grids. The clients can essentially delegate their requests to the servers. This approach results in a very highly scalable model, but with the disadvantage of requiring an additional network hop. To mitigate the additional network hop latency, you can use

the IDDM systems edge-caching facility to localize the data needed, and manage data consistency through a prudent data-refresh cycle, eviction policy, or a data-push policy when new data is made available.

- Hub-Spoke Connected Distributed Systems: Any P2P distributed systems could be configured to replicate all or a portion of their managed data using asynchronous store and forward gateways to one or more remote distributed systems, over a LAN or WAN. P2P distributed system design requires that the peers are tightly coupled and share common high-speed network backplanes. Traffic among peers is generally synchronous and can be very chatty. To distribute data across members that span WAN boundaries, an IDDM system can use a gateway feature for effective asynchronous replication across the WAN. A gateway mechanism essentially queues data updates to various data regions and then effectively replicates them to the interested remote systems.

10.16.9 Flexible and Dynamic Distributed Cache Groups

Advanced IDDM systems allow for members (distributed Java applications) that host data to connect to each member in a P2P network to form a distributed system. Further, IDDM systems offer the ability to dynamically change group membership, where members can join or leave the distributed system at any time without causing application downtime. However, depending on the size of the data heap within that node and how much of it needs to be replicated to other members in the distributed system, there may be some impact-to-transaction speed as the other nodes try to synchronize data in order to not lose any information. This ability to dynamically alter capacity is the most important characteristic that allows Java applications to be built without over-provisioning for peak demands while still maintaining good SLAs. Members can discover each other by either subscribing to a common multicast channel or using a TCP-based discovery service.

10.16.10 Failure Detection with IDDM Systems

When enterprise Java application instances that are part of the distributed network membership fail to respond, it is important for other services to detect the failure quickly and seamlessly transition all of the other clients to other available application instances. Modern IDDM systems have these features and can greatly aid in delivering better application uptime SLAs.

Figure 48 shows how the traditional enterprise application with relational database shown in Figure 47 can be retrofitted with Gem-Fire to improve overall scalability and latency.

With an IDDM system such as vFabric GemFire, data is kept in memory, and applications don't have to cross another network hop to get the needed data. Having data in closer proximity to the application vastly improves horizontal scalability and transactional response times.

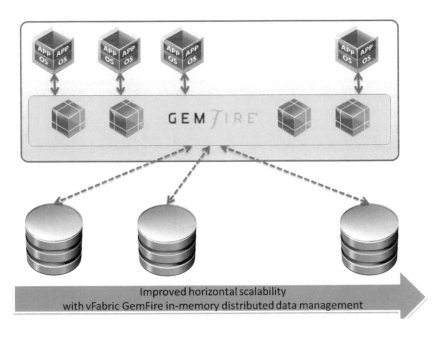

Figure 48: *Shows an improved horizontal scalability using GemFire in-memory distributed data*

IDDM systems provide solutions for many of the challenges of traditional databases. VMware vFabric GemFire is a production-proven IDDM system that is capable of providing highly scalable and available distributed data for your enterprise Java applications. With GemFire you can achieve faster response times and realize the cost benefits of utilizing commodity hardware.

For additional information about vFabric GemFire, see: *GemFire: Elastic Data Management for Virtualized and Cloud-based Applications* (http://www.vmware.com/go/gemfire).

Chapter 11

Troubleshooting Primer

Troubleshooting problems with enterprise Java applications involve the investigation of each of the tiers (the load-balancer tier, the Web server tier, the Java-application server tier, and the DB server tier) and vSphere. VMware vSphere, in turn, has a dependency on networking and storage. The next few sections provide information about how to begin troubleshooting, and effective utilities you can use.

11.1 Open a Support-request Ticket

If you suspect the VMware vSphere is not configured optimally and is cause of the bottleneck, file a support request (http://www.vmware.com/support/contacts/file-sr.html). In addition, you may want to do the following:

Follow the troubleshooting steps outlined in the performance-troubleshooting guide for ESX4.0: http://communities.vmware.com/docs/DOC-10352.

Verify that you have applied all of the best practices discussed in Chapter 6: Enterprise Java on VMware Best Practices

Run the vm-support utility. Execute the following command at the service console:

```
vm-support -s
```

This collects necessary information so that VMware can help diagnose the problem. It is best to run this command at the time when the symptoms occur.

11.2 Troubleshooting Techniques for vSphere with esxtop

11.2.1 Performance Guides and References

Performance Troubleshooting: http://communities.vmware.com/docs/DOC-10352

Interpreting esxtop: http://communities.vmware.com/docs/DOC-11812

11.2.2 esxtop Primer

See *Interpreting esxtop Statistics (http://communities.vmware.com/docs/DOC-11812)* for detailed information about metrics. The following table summarizes some of the metrics you may use when troubleshooting. However for a most common set of metrics used during troubleshooting, refer to Table 7 - **Summary of Common esxtop Metrics**

Table 7: *Summary of Common esxtop Metrics*

Display	Metric	Threshold	Description
CPU	%RDY	10	Over-provisioning of vCPU, excessive usage of vSMP or a limit (check %MLMTD) has been set. This %RDY value is the sum of all vCPUs %RDY for a VM. For example, if the max value of %RDY of 1-vCPU is 100 percent and 4-vCPU is 400 percent. If %RDY is twenty for 1-vCPU then this is problematic, as it means 1-vCPU is waiting 20 percent of the time for VMkernel to schedule it.

CPU	%CSTP	3	Excessive usage of vSMP. Decrease amount of vCPUs for this particular VM.
CPU	%MLMTD	0	If larger than zero the worlds are being throttled. Possible cause is a limit on CPU.
CPU	%SWPWT	5	VM waiting on swapped pages to be read from disk. You may have overcommitted memory.
MEM	MCTLSZ	1	If larger than zero, host is forcing VM to inflate balloon driver to reclaim memory as the host is overcommitted.
MEM	SWCUR	1	If larger than zero, host has swapped memory pages in the past. You may have overcommitted.
MEM	SWR/s	1	If larger than zero, host is actively reading from swap. This is caused by excessive memory overcommitment.
MEM	SWW/s	1	If larger than zero, host is actively writing to swap. This is caused by excessive memory overcommitment.

Display	Metric	Threshold	Description
MEM	N%L	80	If less than eighty, VM experiences poor NUMA locality. If a VM has memory size greater than the amount of memory local to each processor, the ESX scheduler does not attempt to use NUMA optimizations for that VM.
NETWORK	%DRPTX	1	Dropped packages transmitted, hardware is overworked due to high network utilization.
NETWORK	%DRPRX	1	Dropped packages received, hardware is overworked due to high network utilization.
DISK	GAVG	25	Look at DAVG and KAVG as GAVG = DAVG + KAVG.
DISK	DAVG	25	At this level you have disk latency that is likely to be caused by storage array.
DISK	KAVG	2	Disk latency caused by the VMkernel. High KAVG usually means queuing. Check QUED.
DISK	QUED	1	Queue has maxed out. Possibly queue depth is set too low. Check with array vendor for optimal queue value.

DISK	ABRTS/s	1	Aborts issued by VM because storage is not responding. For Windows VMs this happens after sixty-second default. Can be caused by path failure, or storage array Is not accepting IO.
DISK	RESET/s	1	The number of commands resets per second.

NOTE: if you are on ESXi which doesn't have service console you can use vSphere management Assistant vMA, found here: http://www.vmware.com/support/developer/vima/, and a handy resxtop vCLI reference here: https://www.vmware.com/pdf/vsphere4/r41/vsp4_41_vcli_inst_script.pdf

11.3 Java Troubleshooting Primer

Refer to your JVM documentation for troubleshooting guides.

The following sections provide information about how to begin troubleshooting. Information is given about some severe Java-application problems that are GC/memory-leakage-related, and some that are thread-contention-based. For JDBC-based errors, refer to the JDBC driver provided to you by the database vendor. Of particular importance for performance are errors leading to OutofMemory, Stackoverflow, and Thread Deadlock.

11.3.1 Java Memory-problem Troubleshooting

Consider an example where you observe load increases and decreases over a period of time. If memory continues to build without reclamation (in the worst case), or a GC reclamation occurs but not everything is reclaimed, you may have a memory leak. This is very likely if these symptoms persist to a point where the application suffers from an OutofMemory error. In this case you need to investigate the GC frequency and setting.

To turn on GC verbose mode:

- o **verbose:gc:** Prints basic information about GC to the standard output.
- o **-XX:+PrintGCTimeStamps:** Prints the times that GC executes.
- o **-XX:+PrintGCDetails:** Prints statistics about different regions of memory in the JVM.
- o **-Xloggc:<file>:** Logs the results of GC in the specified file.

Re-inspect the **-Xmx,-Xms,-Xss** settings.

If you're using JDK 6, you can use a tool called **jmap** on any platform. Running **jmap** may add additional load on your environment, so plan for the best time to run it.

If you're using JDK 5, remember the following:

- o If you're running Linux with JDK 5 you can use jmap.
- o If you're using JDK 5 update 14 or later, you can use the **-XX:+HeapDumpOnCtrlBreak** option when starting JVM, then use the Ctrl+Break key combination on Windows to dump the heap.

11.3.2 Java Thread-contention Problem

If you suspect that your enterprise Java application is suffering from long pauses, or just has general response-time issues to the point where the JVM needs to be restarted to resolve the issue, you may need to also inspect the Java thread dump. You can obtain a Java thread dump by pressing Ctrl+Break for a Windows OS or in Linux by issuing **Kill -3** on the Java process ID. It is important to take the thread dump right at the point where problematic symptoms appear. This is especially true if you are conducting a benchmark load test—take the thread dump at max peak load, and inspect the behavior of the various application threads.

There are many widely used thread-analysis tools that interpret the thread dump and highlight in red the hot threads or threads waiting for a lock. You can begin your code investigation from that point and follow the call stack.

```
"[ACTIVE] ExecuteThread: '20' for queue: 'xyzAppServer.kernel.Default (self-tuning)'"
  daemon prio=1 tid=0x082e1950 nid=0x2f9d runnable [0x7c96d000..0x7c96dec0]
        at java.net.SocketInputStream.socketRead0(Native Method)
        at java.net.SocketInputStream.read(SocketInputStream.java:129)
        at xyzAppServer.jdbc.xyzDB.net8.XyzDBDataProvider.getArrayOfBytesFromSocket(Unknown Source)
        at xyzAppServer.jdbc.xyzDB.net8.XyzDBDataProvider.readFirstPacketInBuffer(Unknown Source)
        at xyzAppServer.jdbc.xyzDB.net8.XyzDBDataProvider.readPacket(Unknown Source)
        at xyzAppServer.jdbc.xyzDB.net8.XyzDBDataProvider.receive(Unknown Source)
        at xyzAppServer.jdbc.xyzDB.net8.XyzDBNet8NSPTDAPacket.sendRequest(Unknown Source)
        at xyzAppServer.jdbc.xyzDB.XyzDBImplStatement.execute(Unknown Source)
        at xyzAppServer.jdbc.base.BaseStatement.commonExecute(Unknown Source)
        at xyzAppServer.jdbc.base.BaseStatement.executeInternal(Unknown Source)
        at xyzAppServer.jdbc.base.BaseStatement.execute(Unknown Source)
        - locked <0x8a5b7b38> (a xyzAppServer.jdbc.xyzDB.XyzDBConnection)
        at xyzAppServer.jdbc.wrapper.Statement.execute(Statement.java:400)
        at jsp_servlet.__insert_test.jspService(__insert_test.java:108)
        at xyzAppServer.servlet.jsp.JspBase.service(JspBase.java:34)
        at xyzAppServer.servlet.internal.StubSecurityHelper$ServletServiceAction.run(StubSecurityHelper.java:226)
        at xyzAppServer.servlet.internal.StubSecurityHelper.invokeServlet(StubSecurityHelper.java:124)
        at xyzAppServer.servlet.internal.ServletStubImpl.execute(ServletStubImpl.java:283)
        at xyzAppServer.servlet.internal.ServletStubImpl.execute(ServletStubImpl.java:175)
        at xyzAppServer.servlet.internal.WebAppServletContext$ServletInvocationAction.run(WebAppServletContext.java:3370)
        at xyzAppServer.security.acl.internal.AuthenticatedSubject.doAs(AuthenticatedSubject.java:321)
        at xyzAppServer.security.service.SecurityManager.runAs(Unknown Source)
        at xyzAppServer.servlet.internal.WebAppServletContext.securedExecute(WebAppServletContext.java:2117)
        xyzAppServer.servlet.internal.WebAppServletContext.execute(WebAppServletContext.java:2023)
        at at xyzAppServer.servlet.internal.ServletRequestImpl.run(ServletRequestImpl.java:1359)
        at xyzAppServer.work.ExecuteThread.execute(ExecuteThread.java:200)
        at xyzAppServer.work.ExecuteThread.run(ExecuteThread.java:172)
```

Figure 49: *Shows a thread-lock example you can drill down to a "locked-state" thread and inspect*

Chapter 12

FAQ—Enterprise Java Applications on vSphere

"Why would I choose to virtualize enterprise Java applications?"

Improve the efficiency and availability of IT resources and applications through virtualization

Start by eliminating the old "one server, one application" model and run multiple virtual machines on each physical machine

Free your IT administrators from spending so much time managing servers rather than innovating. About 70 percent of a typical IT budget in a non-virtualized datacenter goes towards just maintaining the existing infrastructure, with little left for innovation.

"What use cases are applicable when considering Virtualizing enterprise Java applications?"

Enhanced Scalability: Gain capacity on time, ability to handle load change, dynamic vertical and horizontal scalability, and pooled resources

Optimal Availability: Guard against host failure, zero-downtime deployment, VMware HA via DRS pool

Business Continuity: Execute an automated disaster-recovery plan via VMware vCenter™ Site Recovery Manager (SRM), fast vendor-storage replication

Enhanced Manageability: Achieve cost reduction, all tiers virtualized in one platform, cost reduction through resource efficiency, define clear roles

"What is the return on investment (ROI)?"

This depends on your infrastructure platform and how it is configured. It is not uncommon for VMware customers to report saving in excess of 50 percent. VMware provides an ROI calculator to help you calculate your ROI: http://roitco.vmware.com/vmw/index.html.

"Why choose VMware?"

Gartner said the following:

VMware is in the Leaders Quadrant of the Magic Quadrant for x86 server virtualization infrastructure.

The x86 server-virtualization infrastructure market is a foundation for two extremely important market trends: infrastructure modernization and cloud computing.

Virtualization is enabling a fundamental change in how enterprises manage, deploy, and deliver IT.

x86 architecture server virtualization is now considered a mainstream trend (roughly 25 percent of the market is penetrated), and the strategic path from server virtualization to cloud computing is becoming more apparent to enterprises.

"Are there any performance issues?"

No. Refer to a case study conducted by HP running WebSphere on vSphere: http://www.vmware.com/resources/techresources/10095

Depending on the number of cores or virtual CPUs allocated, the VMware ESX 4.0 virtual environment in some cases exceeds the performance of a physical environment, as shown in 2-cores and 4-cores configurations of about 4 percent and 6 percent, respectively

"What are the key benefits and features of VMware vSphere?"

Key benefits and features of vSphere are discussed in the following: http://www.vmware.com/files/pdf/key_features_vsphere.pdf

"What is SpringSource?"

The Spring Framework is comprised of several modules that provide a range of services:

Inversion of control container: A configuration of application components and lifecycle management of Java objects.

Aspect-oriented programming: A system that enables implementation of crosscutting routines.

Data access: A system that allows working with relational database-management systems on the Java platform using JDBC and object-relational mapping tools.

Transaction management: A system that unifies several transaction-management APIs and coordinates transactions for Java objects.

Model-view-controller: A HTTP and servlet-based framework providing hooks for extension and customization.

Remote access framework: A configurative RPC-style export and import of Java objects over networks supporting RMI, CORBA, and HTTP-based protocols including Web services (SOAP).

Convention-over-configuration: A rapid application-development solution for Spring-based enterprise applications offered in the Spring Roo module.

Batch processing: A framework for high-volume processing featuring reusable functions including logging/tracing, transaction management, job-processing statistics, job restart, skip, and resource management.

Authentication and authorization: A configurable security process that supports a range of standards, protocols, tools, and practices via the Spring Security sub-project (formerly Acegi Security System for Spring).

Remote management: A configurative exposure and management of Java objects for local or remote configuration via JMX.

Messaging: A configurative registration of message listener objects for transparent message consumption from message queues via JMS; improvement of message sending over standard JMS APIs

Testing: Support classes for writing unit tests and integration tests.

GemFire: An in-memory distributed data-management platform that pools memory, CPU, network, and optionally local disk across multiple processes to manage application objects and behaviour. Using dynamic replication and data-partitioning techniques, GemFire Enterprise offers continuous availability, high performance, and linear scalability for data-intensive applications without compromising on data consistency, even under failure conditions. In addition to being a distributed data container, it is an active data-management system that uses an optimized low-latency distribution layer for reliable, asynchronous event notifications and guaranteed message delivery.

RabbitMQ: A complete and highly reliable enterprise messaging system based on the emerging AMQP standard. It is licensed under open source and has a platform-neutral distribution, plus platform-specific packages and bundles for easy installation.

tc Server: An enhanced, enterprise-class version of Tomcat that provides better security, deployment flexibility, and manageability to environments that have more than one hundred Java-application server instances where complexity and manageability are a cost concern.

Hyperic: A system to monitor and manage every element of your Web and enterprise-application infrastructure, with top-down visibility into the performance of Web apps regardless of location, whether it be the datacenter, a virtual environment, or the cloud.

"Do I have to code Java differently when running on vSphere?"

Coding practices don't change for Java on vSphere versus Java on native.

All tuning that you would have done for your Java on native is reusable for Java on vSphere.

While most Java workloads virtualize very readily, there are instances for very high transactions where there may be CPU and memory constraints.

Refer to the *Enterprise Java Applications on VMware – Best Practices Guide* white paper for guidance: http://www.vmware.com/resources/techresources/1087

"Are there any Java best practices for vSphere?"

Yes. Refer to *Enterprise Java Applications on VMware – Best Practices Guide* for guidance: http://www.vmware.com/resources/techresources/1087.

"How would you achieve vertical scalability of enterprise Java applications running on vSphere?"

Vertical scalability features of vSphere allows for compute resources to be adjusted at any time without need for redesign.

"How would you achieve horizontal scalability of enterprise Java applications running on vSphere?"

Horizontal scalability enables you to rapidly create new VMs and have them service traffic to meet your demands.

"How would you guard against server hardware failure when running enterprise Java applications on vSphere?"

VMware High Availability (HA) can relocate the Java-application server to another host that is active, thus minimizing downtime and disruption to service levels.

"How would you achieve high availability of enterprise Java applications running on vSphere?"

You can achieve optimal high availability via VMware DRS, which can be used to balance workloads automatically. VMware HA and DRS with minimal configuration changes can provide a robust availability solution.

"How many JVMs can I stack on a single VM and how many vCPUs should the VM use?"

This depends on your application's transactional throughput. VMware recommends that you performance load test your application to determine your optimal ratio for the number of JVMs, number of VMs, and number of vCPUs on each VM. Also refer to the *Enterprise Java Applications on VMware – Best Practices Guide*: http://www.vmware.com/resources/techresources/1087. Regardless, of VM size you settle on, for example ranging from 2vCPU to 8vCPU, it is always advisable for tier-1 enterprise level Java applications that are carrying serious workloads to maintain a 1 JVM to 2 vCPU ratio. This implies if you settle on 4vCPU VMs, then potentially you could have 2 JVMs on this VM and still adhere to the ratio of 1 JVM to 2 vCPU. Prime reason for this ratio is to allow ample cycles for GC to use first vCPU, while the second vCPU can handle regular user transactions. One of the most common configurations for enterprise Java applications is 1 JVM with 4G heap using a *gencon* type of GC policy, running on 2 vCPU VM with about 5G of memory reservation. Any additional VMs would be introduced in a horizontal scale out fashion with this common configuration. In general horizontal scalability is the preferred architecture as discussed through various chapters of this book.

"Which application servers have been proven on vSphere in production?"

There is not a specific application server that works better with vSphere—all are good candidates. As many VMware customers have demonstrated, their Java environments virtualize very well in dev, test, and production. We find the most commonly used application servers are Oracle Weblogic, IBM WebSphere, JBoss, Tomcat, and SpringSource tc Server, which are all good examples of easily Virtualizable application servers, along with many others.

"What kind of testing has been done to validate running Weblogic on vSphere?"

Multiple performance studies have been conducted at VMware labs over the past several years. These studies show good linear scalability in performance of test applications on Weblogic Server. As you increase the number of virtual machines with instances of Weblogic Server in each one, a building block approach can be followed to scale up your application's user population.

"Which Web servers have been proven on vSphere in production?"

It has been demonstrated that both Apache Web server and Microsoft IIS run well on vSphere and in production.

"Enterprise Java application platforms are multitier. Which tiers does it make sense to virtualize first?"

At high level, we classify the enterprise Java-applications platform into the following tiers:

- Load Balancer Tier
- Web Server Tier
- Java Application Server Tier
- DB Tier

We do not recommend any particular order, and there are VMware customers that virtualize all of the tiers. However, we do see a growing trend where migrations are done on phases as follows:

- Phase One: Migrate the Web Server Tier to run on vSphere.
- Phase Two: Migrate the Java Application Server to run on vSphere.
- Phase Three: Migrate the DB Server Tier to run on vSphere.
- Phase Four: Optionally migrate the Load Balancer Tier to run on vSphere via load-balancer third-party virtual appliances that run on vSphere.

"How does vSphere help with business continuity for enterprise Java applications?"

VMware vCenter Site Recovery Manager does the following:

- Provides failover to secondary site
- Automates your recovery plans
- Allows a fast storage-replication adaptor
- Recovers multiple sites into a single shared recovery site.
- Simulates and tests the recovery plan
- Provides a powerful API for further scripting (http://www. vmware.com/support/developer/srm-api/srm_10_api.pdf)

"If I have a problem with Oracle Weblogic Server running on VMware, who should I call for support?"

Oracle provides best-effort support for Weblogic Server running on VMware software. Customers can initiate a support call with either Oracle for Weblogic-related issues or with VMware support for VMware virtualization-related issues. The best and quickest way to isolate a problem is to have VMware and Oracle support teams working together jointly to resolve an issue.

"If I have a problem with IBM WebSphere Server running on VMware virtual infrastructure, who should I call for support?"

General software support for IBM SWG products in a VMware environment:
http://www-01.ibm.com/support/docview.wss?&uid=wws1e333 ce0912f7b152852571f60074d175
VMware product support information for IBM WebSphere Application Server products:
http://www-01.ibm.com/support/docview. wss?uid=swg21242532
Support statement for WebSphere Virtual Enterprise (XD) 6.1:
http://publib.boulder.ibm.com/infocenter/wxdinfo/v6r1/index. jsp?topic=/com.ibm.websphere.ops.doc/info/prodovr/changes.html

"What about licensing?"

- For vSphere licensing contact VMware Sales at http://www.vmware.com/contact/contact_sales.html.
- For licensing and application servers, contact the specific application-server vendor.
- Oracle Weblogic: The following provides additional information on support, licensing, and pricing.
  - General software support for Oracle products in a VMware environment; MetaLink 269212.1 on the Oracle partner website:
  - http://myoraclesupport.oracle.com or http://metalink.oracle.com
  - You must be registered as a support user to get to the MetaLink document.
- IBM WebSphere:
  - Pricing policies for IBM software on virtualized platforms, including VMware: http://www-01.ibm.com/software/lotus/passportadvantage/Counting_Software_licenses_using_specific_virtualization_technologies.html
  - Pricing policies for IBM support:
  - **http://www-01.ibm.com/software/lotus/passportadvantage/pvu_licensing_for_customers.html**

"Are there any additional references for IBM WebSphere running on vSphere?"

- IBM WebSphere V7 and VMware ESX 3.5 performance and scalability study:
  - ftp://ftp.software.ibm.com/software/webservers/appserv/WASV7_VMware_performance
- Best practices for deploying VMware ESX 4.0 and IBM WebSphere Application Server 7.0 on HP ProLiant DL380 G6 servers:

- o http://h20195.www2.hp.com/V2/GetPDF.aspx/4AA0-2988ENW.pdf
- IBM WebSphere Rapid Provisioning with VMware virtualization infrastructure:
  - o http://h20195.www2.hp.com/V2/GetPDF.aspx/4AA0-2988ENW.pdf
  - o IBM WebSphere Hypervisor Edition (built for VMware platform using VOE/OVF standards):
  - o http://www.youtube.com/watch?v=MXVcCgX-jYg
  - o IBM WebSphere CloudBurst Appliance (built for VMware platform using VOE/OVF standards):
  - o http://www.youtube.com/watch?v=udh4d0TIXGI

How can I get additional information about running IBM WebSphere on vSphere?

If you have a new WebSphere Application Server project and are ready to get started Virtualizing with VMware vSphere:

- View VMworld WebSphere presentations from IBM:
  - o VMworld 2011: Session BCA 1950 – Proven Production Methods of Running Enteprise Java on VMware (Includes a Websphere case study)
  - o VMworld 2008: Session EA 2538 – Using IBM WebSphere Family Products with VMware.
  - o VMworld 2009: Session EA 3820 – Using WebSphere with vSphere.
- Download the latest IBM and HP performance whitepapers:
  - o ftp://ftp.software.ibm.com/software/webservers/appserv/WASV7_VMware_performance_1.23.pdf
  - o http://h20195.www2.hp.com/V2/GetPDF.aspx/4AA0-4618ENW.pdf

Are there any customer references?

Here is a partial list of VMware customers who have already been successful in Virtualizing applications on Weblogic Server.

- **First American Financial Group:** https://www.vmware.com/files/pdf/partners/first_american_corp_cs_091207.pdf
- **I2 Technologies India: https://www.vmware.com/files/pdf/customers/apac_in_08Q1_ss_vmw_i2_technologies_english.pdf**
- VMware Session on Oracle E-Business Suite from VMworld 2009 (this can be viewed without a password): http://www.vmworld.com/docs/DOC-3624

Here is a partial list of VMware customers who have already been successful in virtualizing applications on WebSphere Application Server:

- Ohio Mutual Insurance Group (OMIG):
- http://www.vmware.com/files/pdf/customers/08Q4_isv_vmw_OMIG_english.pdf
- T-Systems Austria:
- http://www.vmware.com/files/pdf/customers/06Q4_cs_vmw_T-systems_Austria_English.pdf
- First Marblehead:
- http://www.vmware.com/files/pdf/customers/09Q2_cs_vmw_First_Marblehead_english.pdf

"With UNIX-based hardware, I have very large machines running all of my Java applications. What should be my migration-sizing strategy, and what are the VMware vSphere maximums that I need to know about?"

One of the most important steps is to conduct a load test to help you determine the ideal individual-VM size and how many JVMs you can stack up (vertical scalability). Based on this repeatable building-block VM you can scale-out to determine what is best for your application traffic profile.

Know the VMware vSphere maximums. See Configuration Maximums: VMware vSphere 4.1 http://www.vmware.com/pdf/vsphere4/r41/vsp_41_config_max.pdf.

NOTE: the maximums below are for VMware vSphere 4.1, and it is anticipated these will be changed in future releases. Always refer to configuration maximums on the VMware site as to the latest maximums. But suffice to say that as of the writing of this book, the maximums quoted here are current for vSphere 4.1. The most notable changes within vSphere5 will be the ability to create up to 32vCPU VMs, and memory usage of up to 1TB. Also unique to vSphere5 is the fact that the NUMA architecture will be exposed to the Guest OS so that some very large database type of workloads could take advantage of it. In vSphere4.1 as mentioned earlier the NUMA architecture details are not exposed to the Guest OS, in the case of Java this shouldn't matter whether you are using vSphere4.1 or vSphere5, the NUMA locality of staying within 2vCPU, 4vCPU, and 8vCPU (assuming the hardware used has NUMA nodes that are that wide) then you are already using ESX scheduler NUMA optimizations without any need for further tuning. You will also not need turn on the -XX:UseNUMA option on the JVM since the ESX scheduler NUMA optimizations are highly effective. If you suspect that you have a NUMA locality problem you can inspect the esxtop parameter N%L, if this is below 100% then your VMs are not NUMA local and you would need to size in accordance of the memory available to your NUMA nodes, along with sizing vCPU within the available cores per socket/NUMA node.

Table 8 provides a summary of maximums for per VM, per Host, and per vCenter.

Table 8: *vSphere 4.1 Configuration Maximums*

vSphere Configuration	Maximum
Per VM	8-vCPUs 255GB 2TB of storage minus 512 bytes
Per Host	512-vCPUs 320 VMs 25-vCPUs per core
Per vCenter	1,000 hosts 10,000 Powered on VMs 15,000 registered VMs 10 Linked vCenter Servers 3,000 hosts in linked vCenter servers 30,000 powered on VMs in linked vCenter Servers 50,000 registered VMs in linked vCenter Servers 100 concurrent vSphere Clients 400 hosts per datacenter

"What decisions must be made due to virtualization?"

You have to determine the size of the repeatable building-block VM. This is established by benchmarking, along with total scale-out factor. Determine how many concurrent users each single vCPU configuration of your application can handle, and extrapolate that to your production traffic to determine the overall compute-resource requirement. Having a symmetrical building block (for example, every VM having the same number of vCPUs), helps keep load distribution from your load balancer even. Essentially, your benchmarking test helps you determine how large a single VM should be (vertical scalability) and how many of these VMs you will need (horizontal scalability).

You need to pay special attention to scale-out factor, and see up to what point it is linear within your application running on top of VMware. Enterprise Java applications are multi-tiered, and bottle-necks can appear at any point along the scale-out performance line and quickly cause non-linear results. The assumption of linear scal-ability may not always be true, and it is essential to load test a prepro-duction replica (production to be) of your environment to accurately size for you traffic.

"I have conducted extensive GC sizing and tuning for our current enterprise Java application running on physical. Do I have to adjust anything related to sizing when moving this Java application to a virtualized environment?"

No. All tuning that you would perform for your Java application on physical is transferrable to your virtual environment. However, because virtualization projects are typically about driving a high-consolidation ratio, it is advisable that you conduct adequate load testing to establish your ideal compute-resource configuration for individual VMs, number of JVMs within a VM, and overall number of VMs on the ESX host.

Additionally, because this type of migration involves an OS/plat-form change as well as a JVM vendor change, it is advisable to adhere to the various design and sizing, best practices, and tuning details dis-cussed throughout this book.

"How many and what size of virtual machines will I need?"

This depends on the nature of your application. We most often see 2-vCPU VMs as a common building block for Java applications. One of the guidelines is to tune your system for more scale-out as opposed to scale-up. This rule is not absolute, as it depends on your organization's architectural best practices. Smaller, more scaled-out VMs may provide better overall architecture, but you will incur addi-tional guest-OS licensing costs. If this is a constraint then you can tune towards larger 4-vCPU VMs and stack more JVMs on them.

"What is the correct number of JVMs per virtual machine?"

There is no one definite answer. This largely depends on the nature of your application. The benchmarking you conduct can determine the limit of the number of JVMs that can be stacked up on a single VM.

The more JVMs you put on a single VM the more JVM overhead and cost of initializing a JVM is incurred. Alternately, instead of stacking up multiple JVMs within a VM, you can instead increase the JVM size vertically by adding more threads and heap size. This can be achieved if your JVM is within an application server such as Tomcat. Then, instead of increasing the number of JVMs you can increase the number of concurrent threads available and resources that a single Tomcat JVM services for your n-number of applications deployed and their concurrent requests per second. The limitation of how many applications you can stack up within a single application-server instance/JVM is bounded by how large you can afford your JVM heap size to be and performance. The trade-off of very large JVM heap size beyond 4GB needs to be tested for performance and GC-cycle impact. This concern is not specific to virtualization, as it equally applies to physical-server setup.

Regardless, of VM size you settle on, for example ranging from 2vCPU to 8vCPU, it is always advisable for tier-1 enterprise level Java applications that are carrying serious workloads to maintain a 1 JVM to 2 vCPU ratio. This implies if you settle on 4vCPU VMs, then potentially you could have 2 JVMs on this VM and still adhere to the ratio of 1 JVM to 2 vCPU. Prime reason for this ratio is to allow ample cycles for GC to use first vCPU, while the second vCPU can handle regular user transactions.   One of the most common configurations for enterprise Java applications is 1 JVM with 4G heap using a *gencon* type of GC policy, running on 2 vCPU VM with about 5G of memory reservation. Any additional VMs would be introduced in a horizontal scale out fashion with this common configuration. In general horizontal scalability is the preferred architecture as discussed through various chapters of this book.

"We would like to use the full logical CPU capacity of a host and take full advantage of HT."

Let's take the example of a Dell server R810, dual 8-core machine with HT enabled. It means there are sixteen physical CPUs, and with HT enabled the count is thirty-two logical CPUs. The ideal case here would be to configure multiple VMs, choosing from various available vCPU configurations, such as 2-vCPU, 4-vCPU, or 8-vCPU. Aim at adhering to the equation of

Total vCPUs = Physical CPUs + 25%.

In our example here, this means we have

16 Physical CPUs + 25% * 16 = 20-vCPUs approximately.

Now this is not a cast-in-stone rule, and you can actually go higher than this in terms of adding, for example, three VMs with each being at 8-vCPU, for a total of 24-vCPUs, and you may find the overall host CPU utilization still within the acceptable range for your setup. But anything beyond this you will start to encroach on the limits of the host.

NOTE: Even though the processor has hyper-threading, scheduling more frequently does not guarantee that the VM will catch up. This is because the amount of CPU resources received by the vCPU is affected by the activity on the other logical processor on the same physical core. To guarantee the vCPU that is behind can catch up, ESX will sometimes not schedule VMs on the other logical processor, effectively leaving it idle. Refer to http://kb.vmware.com/kb/1020233

List of Figures and Tables

Glossary

AMQP

This is the Advanced Message Queuing Protocol (AMQP) is an open standard application layer protocol for message-oriented middleware. The protocol has features such as messaging, queuing, routing both point-to-point and publish-and-subscribe, in addition to reliability and security.

Ballooning

Ballooning is the name given to the memory reclamation process invoked by the balloon driver. The balloon driver, also known as the vmmemctl driver, collaborates with the server to reclaim pages that are considered least valuable by the guest operating system. It essentially acts like a native program in the operating system that requires more and more memory. The driver uses a proprietary ballooning technique that provides predictable performance that closely matches the behavior of a native system under similar memory constraints. This technique effectively increases or decreases memory pressure on the guest operating system, causing the guest to invoke its own native memory management algorithms. You can refer to the following vSphere memory management paper for additional details: http://www.vmware.com/files/pdf/perf-vsphere-memory_management.pdf

CPU Overcommit

This is where you are allocating more virtual CPU resources than what is physically available on the ESX Host, for further reading refer to vSphere Best Practices Paper: http://www.vmware.com/pdf/Perf_Best_Practices_vSphere4.0.pdf

DRS

vSphere Distributed Resource Scheduler and vSphere DRS continuously balances computing capacity in resource pools to deliver the performance, scalability and availability not possible with physical infrastructure. DRS uses VMotion to move VMs around in order to more fairly distribute workloads.

Dependency Injection

Dependency injection is a specific form of inversion of control where the concern being inverted is the process of obtaining the needed dependency. The term was first coined by Martin Fowler to describe the mechanism more clearly. **Dependency injection** in object-oriented programming is a technique that is used to supply an external dependency or reference, to a software component. In technical terms, it is a design pattern that separates behavior from dependency resolution, thus decoupling highly dependent components. *Instead of components having to request dependencies, they are given, or injected, into the component.*

GC

Garbage Collection (GC) is a mechanism provided by the Java Virtual machine (JVM) to reclaim heap space from objects which are eligible to be garbage collected. Java objects that become de-referenced, i.e. no longer used are eligible for garbage collection. NOTE: Java objects are born in the young generation segment of the JVM, and are copied to survivor spaces, should they survive a minor garbage collection, if they continue to survive other minor collection they will be copied to the tenured space, where eventually a full GC of the tenured space will collect them should the objects become de-referenced, i.e. objects are no longer used by the application.

Guest OS

This is the either Linux or Windows based operating systems that are installed on the Virtual Machine.

Host

A Host in VMware terminology is a Server Hardware that is running VMware's ESX bare metal hypervisor. It is a "host" for Virtual Machines to run on.

IOC

In software engineering, Inversion of Control (IoC) is an abstract principle describing an aspect of some software architecture designs in which the flow of control of a system is inverted in comparison to procedural programming. In traditional programming the flow of the business logic is controlled by a central piece of code, which calls reusable subroutines that perform specific functions. Using Inversion of Control this "central control" design principle is abandoned. The caller's code deals with the program's execution order, but the business knowledge is encapsulated by the called subroutines.

In practice, Inversion of Control is a style of software construction where reusable generic code controls the execution of problem-specific code. It carries the strong connotation that the reusable code and the problem-specific code are developed independently, which often results in a single integrated application.

Java Virtual Machine

The Java Virtual Machine (JVM) is a virtual machine capable of executing Java bytecode.

Memory Overcommit

This is where you have allocated more RAM than is physically available on the host

Memory Reservation

The minimum amount of physical memory guaranteed to be made available to the VM at all times. If this requested reserved memory is not available upon VM startup, the VM will simply not start. A success-ful startup of the VM means the required memory was reserved.

Large Memory Pages

In addition to the usual 4KB memory pages, ESX also makes 2MB memory pages available (commonly referred to as "large pages"). By default ESX assigns these 2MB machine memory pages to guest op-erating systems that request them, giving the guest operating system the full advantage of using large pages. The use of large pages results in reduced memory management overhead and can therefore in-crease hypervisor performance. If an operating system or application can benefit from large pages on a native system, that operating system or application can potentially achieve a similar performance improve-ment on a virtual machine backed with 2MB machine memory pages. Consult the documentation for your operating system and applica-tion to determine how to configure them each to use large memory pages. More information about large page support can be found in the performance study entitled Large Page Performance (available at http://www.vmware.com/resources/techresources/1039)

NUMA

Non-Uniform Memory Access (**NUMA**) is a computer memory design used in multiprocessors, where the memory access time de-pends on the memory location relative to a processor. Under NUMA, a processor can access its own local memory faster than non-local memory, that is, memory local to another processor or memory shared between processors.

vApp

A vApp is a collection of virtual machines (and potentially other vApp containers) that are operated and monitored as a unit. From a management perspective, a multi-tiered vApp acts a lot like a virtual machine object. It has power operations, networks, datastores, and its resource usage can be configured.

Virtual Machine (VM)

A virtual machine is a software implementation of a machine, i.e. computer that executes programs like a physical machine would. VMs can be created with variant compute resources, such as Virtual CPU, referred to as vCPU, RAM, and Storage.

VMotion

vMotion technology, deployed in production by 80% of VMware customers leverage the complete virtualization of servers, storage, and networking to move an entire running virtual machine instantaneously from one server to another. vMotion uses the VMware cluster file system to control access to a virtual machine's storage. During a vMotion, the active memory and precise execution state of a virtual machine is rapidly transmitted over a high speed network from one physical server to another, and access to the virtual machines disk storage is instantly switched to the new physical host. Since the network is also virtualized by the VMware host, the virtual machine retains its network identity and connections, ensuring a seamless migration process.

VMware vCenter

VMware vCenter Server is the simplest, most efficient way to manage VMware vSphere—whether you have ten VMs or tens of thousands of VMs. It provides unified management of all the hosts and VMs in your datacenter from a single console with an aggregate performance monitoring of clusters, hosts and VMs. VMware vCenter Server gives administrators deep insight into the status and configuration of clusters, hosts, VMs, storage, the guest OS and other critical components of a virtual infrastructure—all from one place.

VMware ESX/ESXi

Like its predecessor ESX, ESXi is a "bare-metal" hypervisor, meaning it installs directly on top of the physical server and partitions it into multiple virtual machines that can run simultaneously, sharing the physical resources of the underlying server. VMware introduced ESXi in 2007 to deliver industry-leading performance and scalability while setting a new bar for reliability, security and hypervisor management efficiency.

While both architectures use the same kernel to deliver virtualization capabilities, the ESX architecture also contains a Linux operating system (OS), called "Service Console," that is used to perform local management tasks such as executing scripts or installing third party agents. The Service Console has been removed from ESXi, drastically reducing the hypervisor code-base footprint (less than 150MB vs. ESX's 2GB) and completing the ongoing trend of migrating management functionality from the local command line interface to remote management tools.

VMware vSphere

VMware vSphere, (prior name, VMware Infrastructure 4) is VMware's first cloud operating system, able to manage large pools of virtualized computing infrastructure, including software and hardware.

Index

Made in the USA
Charleston, SC
02 December 2011